Catching Your Breath

ISBN: 978-1-7323807-4-5 (pbck)
        978-1-7323807-1-4 (ebook)
        978-1-7323807-2-1 (audio)

Catching Your Breath

The Sacred Journey from Chaos to Calm

STEVE AUSTIN

ALSO BY THIS AUTHOR

From Pastor to a Psych Ward:
Recovery From a Suicide Attempt is Possible

The Writer's Toolkit:
How to Own and Craft Your Story

Self-Care for the Wounded Soul:
21 Days of Messy Grace

I Love Jesus, But…:
Embracing the Tension between Faith and Mental Health

Get them all at graceismessybooks.com

ENDORSEMENTS

Two things make Steve Austin's voice unique and worth hearing. First, he's been through hell and comes back with the kind of hopefulness that is as contagious as it is compelling. People are always better for having encountered such people. Second, he's candid. He says the thing that so many are thinking but are afraid to say, and shares the details of the story that others would hide—and he does all of that without being smug or self-aggrandizing. On the contrary, Steve's candor is tempered by grace and compassion that makes it safe for others to be honest about what they're experiencing and to also encounter hope. In *Catching Your Breath*, Steve offers himself as a companion to those who feel like they are drowning, not as a lifeguard but as a coach saying "Hey. You can swim!"

—Andre Henry, Managing Editor, RELEVANT Magazine

My friend Steve understands more than most that we are messed-up people living in a messed-up world with other messed-up people. He understands the human condition. He refuses to sugarcoat the depth of his own desperation and need. But he also understands that God meets our messed-up-ness with his mercy over and over and over again. He understands that God loves bad and broken people because bad and broken people are all that there are. He's uncomfortably honest, remarkably compassionate, and beautifully rough around the edges. Thank you for your friendship, Steve. And thank you for this book. Page after page you reminded me that "It is finished."

—Tullian Tchividjian, author of *One-Way Love:*
***Inexhaustible Grace for an Exhausted World* and**
Jesus + Nothing = Everything

Steve Austin is one of the most genuine guys I know. He is sincere, thoughtful, and one of the funniest guys I've met. Steve is brutally honest about his story. He doesn't hold back.

In *Catching Your Breath*, Steve invites you into the darkest and holiest moments of his life with courage and vulnerability. Steve's book is relatable, giving practical advice for those who feel overwhelmed. His advice is real, messy, and hard-won. This is the book Steve was born to write.

As I was reading *Catching Your Breath*, I was convinced that Steve had been reading my mind. Thankfully, he had just the words I needed to hear. I hope you enjoy this book as much as I did.

—Michael Baysinger, host of The Inglorious Pasterds Podcast

In his book, *Catching Your Breath*, Steve Austin meets you where you are. Austin immediately puts himself in your shoes, gently takes your hand, and from there, you're off. From the practical and relatable advice he gives, you can tell he's been there. I would highly recommend this book to a friend who's going through a tough time.

—Sarah Schuster, Mental Health editor at TheMighty.com

Steve Austin has done it again. *Catching Your Breath* is a truth-telling memoir about being truly human. In our "fake-it-till-you-make-it-world" of 24/7 shiny posts that fuel our perfectionism, Austin delivers courageous medicine: we are all broken—and more important, we are all beautiful, valuable, unique, and connected. Instead of hiding, Austin calls us all to the table and asks us to catch our breaths in order to be vulnerable—together. What a gift!

—J. Dana Trent, author of *For Sabbath's Sake*

Steve Austin has written a masterpiece! He gives us permission to be sad and feel again. In a world that demands that we suppress our feelings, Steve unleashes the power of the soul by showing us we can heal from anything life throws at us! I highly recommend this work of art!

—Jeremy Lopez, author and entrepreneur

What a beautiful gift this book is for those of us living in today's world. Steve's wholehearted vulnerability invites us to question the often-glorified and addictive pattern of chaos, constantly going, unhealthy striving, achieving to avoid pain, comparing, and the illusion of control.

We get one sacred life and what we do with this time matters. For this reason, I am deeply grateful for Steve's willingness to share his story as a reminder that we can't always control what happens in life, but we can often control how we respond to others, events, and situations in life. It is in this subtle shift of control that Steve unpacks how we can ultimately move from chaos to calm along this sacred journey.

—Holly K. Oxhandler, PhD, LMSW, Baylor University

Steve's website says "underdogs welcome." He means that! His life embodies grace and compassion for everyone. He was at rock bottom when he attempted suicide; since that day, he's softened and matured and grown and learned and has been sharing his story of messy grace the entire way. If you've ever felt overwhelmed or unsure of how to move forward, I recommend *Catching Your Breath*. Steve's story is real, raw, and relatable.

—J.J. Landis, author of *Some Things You Keep*

A Siberian elder once wrote, "If you don't know the trees you may be lost in the forest, but if you don't know the stories you may be lost in life."

A lot of us feel lost in life because we either don't know or else can't admit to our own story. As a result, life can hurt so much we find ourselves wondering if it's worth it. We feel crippled, as if some kind of highly personalized Kryptonite is slowly destroying us. And there is, a Kryptonite that is emotionally powerful enough to seduce even the strongest willed into believing lies about themselves and others, lies that can cripple and destroy, lies that force us to hide behind gleaming smiles on the outside while inside we feel as if our life is going up in flames and no one else can even hear the fire alarm ringing.

Steve Austin understands that Kryptonite can only be conquered using the superpower of words—the words that we speak to others and the words that we speak to ourselves. In *Catching Your Breath*, he helps the reader learn to use words as a weapon to tell their own story, thus lancing the festering boil of anxiety and neutralizing the power of dark secrets. Most of all, he offers the reader a taste of wildly extravagant grace. If you are among the multitudes who need help just to survive the next 24 hours, this book will be a God-send.

—Dr. Paula Champion Jones, Retired UMC pastor

What strikes me the most about *Catching Your Breath* is Austin's vulnerability, authenticity, and encouragement. Through personal stories and self-reflection, Austin provides a safe place that permits readers to be open and genuinely themselves, secrets and all. This is a book that I would not hesitate to recommend to my clients.

—Erin Reagan, LMHC

In *Catching Your Breath*, Steve Austin has written a treatise for finding our center amidst the frantic pace of today's world.

So many of us live lives that move too quickly; we are expected to keep up in order to succeed. What happens when going with the crowd is anathema to your personal goals in life? Steve Austin recounts experiences that many might relate to. Be still and know that Spirit exists within each of us. We just need to slow our lives down so our dreams can catch up.

I am honored to recommend this book to people who feel burnt out, used up, and lifeless. *Catching Your Breath* can feed your creative spirit again, and provide fuel as you move, at your own pace, going forward.

—Rev. Andrea L. Stoeckel

Have you ever had the feeling that the air is too thick, that it is dense and not filling your lungs correctly? Does it feel like you're drowning in a bottomless pool of water, your legs tiring from treading water? If you're longing for someone to permit you to pause, be still, be silent, and catch your breath, then you ought to read Steve Austin's latest book.

Catching Your Breath urges you to take stock of your life and shed some of that unwanted heaviness. Through personal narrative, plus his training as a life coach, Austin masterfully leads the reader through the seemingly overwhelming task of finding calm, making the transition achievable and maintainable. This book empowers the reader to approach their journey with acceptance, honesty, and patience while journeying toward the calm we all possess. In *Catching Your Breath*, Austin invites you to slow down and rest, while simultaneously empowering you to reach out and grab life by both hands.

—Laura Cass, blogger & mental health advocate

Catching Your Breath is a fearless work in which Austin demonstrates vulnerability and nakedness; showing us his scars so we can begin to be comfortable with our own. His story travels with us to places of deep pain, but his words of encouragement provide a ladder and light for the climb out. The book is a wonderful resource for anyone who has encountered brokenness inflicted by others or self. When you read it, you'll find yourself catching your breath often, and then pausing to breathe deep.

—**Suzanne DeWitt Hall, author of the *Rumplepimple* adventures and *Where True Love Is: An Affirming Devotional for LGBTQI+ Individuals and Their Allies***

For Sue, who has always made space for me.
Thanks for the chicken noodle soup.
Most of all, thanks for being my friend.
It's all grace and gratitude.

CONTENTS

ACKNOWLEDGMENTS

The book you're holding has been a labor of love and a product of community from the very start. When I sent the original 8,000-word essay to my friend, I had no intention of writing another book. What unfolded was something between a divine accident and a story a lifetime in the making. It would not have happened without some incredible people.

Laura Cass (onlymelaura85.wordpress.com), thank you for reading the original essay. Thank you for continuing to compel me to "say more." This book is all your fault. *No, really.*

Stephanie Long (redeemedformore.com), thank you for reading the original essay, too. And for your incredible work with the study guide. I'm so thankful for your friendship and expertise!

Stephanie Gates (awidemercy.com), you are the ruthless unicorn whom I adore. You helped me find my voice a few years ago, and your friendship remains a gift from God.

Sarah Robinson (beautifulbetween.com)—your book is next. I have never felt more clear on who I am and what I think about things like life, faith, and overcoming the darkness. It is all thanks to the work we did together. You are the very best. Thank you!

Ed Bacon (edbacon.co), when I met you, everything started to shift. *Holy shift!* You famously said, "grace just comes," and you are the Grace of God to me. Thank you for being my friend. And thanks for the sammiches and greens, too!

Doris and Judy, I couldn't have asked for better big sisters. Your love and encouragement have done wonders for my soul. Judy, so has your coaching, which got me ready to write this treatise in the first place. Let's sit under the oaks soon!

Beta readers, Kickstarter backers, my Pub friends, and members of the launch group: you're the real heroes. Thank you for affirming my work and pushing me to keep going. *Further up, further in.*

Deep bows to Dr. Holly Oxhandler, Rev. Dr. David P. Gushee, Rev. Andrea Stoeckel, Michael Baysinger, J. Dana Trent, J.J. Landis, Sarah Schuster, Andre Henry, Jeremy Lopez, Tullian Tchividjian, Andie Becker, Suzanne DeWitt Hall, Rev. Paula Champion Jones, Faydra Koenig, and Erin Regan.

Devin Balram (noisetraide.com/devinbalram), your music puts soul to my scattered thoughts. "Weak Sometimes" sits on repeat on my phone most days. I understand how David's music was the only thing that could soothe Saul's troubled soul. I get it. Thank you.

Melinda Martin (melindamartin.me) and Nathan Miller (namwaydesign. com), thank you. You are joys to work with! The way you are able to see what I can only write is such a gift.

Thank you to my precious grandparents, Boss and Nanny. I don't know many folks who get to count their grandparents among their dearest friends—I am doubly blessed. Thanks for teaching me to "saucer and blow it." Thanks for all the movie nights. And thanks for the banana pancakes—we'll have them again one day.

Ben and Cara, you are my world. Thanks for always reminding Daddy of what matters most. You ask the best questions, make me laugh, remind me to play, and always tell the truth. I love you two better than a hog loves slop!

Most important, Lindsey Austin. Your compassion, stubborn love, and abiding friendship have been my anchor through some unthinkable storms. I'm grateful that the girl who said, "huh?" still chooses to love me. I am yours, always. *Fully known, fully loved.*

FOREWORD

"You have an open invitation."

That sentence means you aren't required to make an appointment or give any kind of notice — like a day's notice or a week's notice. No, with an open invitation, friends in need can drop by any time.

Steve Austin is a walking open invitation. "Simply drop by anytime, unannounced, for a visit," his life says. This book is an open invitation, as well. Open it any time, to any page, for a visit.

The openness of the invitation stems in part from Steve being a son of Southern hospitality, but that's only part of his passion for welcoming all at any time. The real, palpable passion in these pages is more profound than his culture's conventions.

Steve Austin's genuinely open invitation stems from his acute awareness of his own wounds. Steve is courageous in sharing his pain with others and knows that new life comes from visiting honestly with other injured people.

To live is to be wounded. New life in the midst of woundedness requires inviting others to see and even touch your wounds. This is what I refer to as, "The Rule of the Soul." Before we use a scripture verse about Jesus's wounds to place a simplistic period on the sentence and walk away, hear me out.

As an Episcopal priest, I re-discover the "Rule of the Soul" any time I preach about my own eight years of psychiatric treatment for Clinical Depression. This chapter of my life opened when I discovered the God of my fundamentalistic Baptist childhood had reached its expiration date; I no longer believed in that kind of God. Every time I mention that painful season of my life in a sermon, people come up afterward to tell me how much it meant to them. The Rule of the Soul is real, and it saves lives. Wherever in your life you are wounded, when you practice hospitality toward other wounded people, you experience new life. And so do they.

This Rule of the Soul gained currency in Christian Pastoral Care circles at the hands of one of the 20th century's spiritual geniuses, Henri Nouwen, in his classic text, *The Wounded Healer*. It is a truth that the poet Rumi taught long before Leonard Cohen wrote that "there's a crack in everything; that's how the light gets in." Rumi had written that your wounds are how the light gets in.

All the world's religions teach us that in addition to joy, blessings, love, and pleasure, life is also suffering. In his book, Nouwen tells the Talmudic story of how you can identify the Messiah. The Messiah, the anointed one, is the wounded one sitting at the city gate among the others who are injured. But as others remove all the bindings from all their wounds at one time, the anointed one unwraps his wounds one at a time. He then redresses each injury, one at a time so he can be ready to move into action when he is needed to care for the wounds of others. That is why Nouwen called his book *The Wounded Healer.*

The issue in life is not whether we have wounds. The point is whether we understand that our wounds can be a source of power for us and others. The issue is not whether or not you have injuries. But are you willing to allow others to touch your wounds, empowering them to lead others toward wholeness, too? Using our wounds is a great delivery system of healing. The great 21st-century leader of the Equal Justice Initiative in Montgomery, Bryan Stevenson, often notes, "The reason I have such commitment to ministering to the broken in our justice system is that I'm broken too!"[1]

The word Henri Nouwen uses for this practice is hospitality. Are you willing to extend hospitality to those who are wounded, allowing them to experience and learn from your woundedness? That hospitality is the difference between your wounds paralyzing or mobilizing you. Can you hospitably make room for other wounded persons in your heart? If so, you will be not paralyzed by your wounds, but mobilized. The issue in life is not whether you have been wounded, but how your scars are acknowledged and used. Will you make room for others to tend to their injuries in your presence?

It's been said that the difference between those who are religious and those who are spiritual is this: religious people are trying to stay out of hell. Spiritual people are those who have already been there.

Steve Austin knows the wounds of hell about which he writes so movingly in this book. In the case of every wound he knows, he has turned that wound into a source of healing power. That is why Steve is one of the most mobilized, energized, walking witnesses of new life I have ever known. Now, fasten your seatbelt and prepare for a hefty dose of new life for yourself in his words.

Ed Bacon
Birmingham, Alabama

April 19, 2018

INTRODUCTION

Hey, God? I sure could use some grace today. Make it messy. Sloppy. Over-flowing. Spread it all over my worn-the-hell-out brain. Remind me that I am loved beyond anything I can comprehend. Because today, nothing much makes sense or helps.

Anxiety is eating me alive. It feels like it is corroding me from the inside out. I know most people think it lives in the brain, and while that may be true, my anxiety likes to vacation in the deepest part of my gut.

And I hate it. I hate it so damn much.

It feels like the inner lining of my stomach has been filled with battery acid and eroding away since Tuesday morning. That's five full days of misery. One hundred and twenty hours and counting of sweating palms, chest pain, and a knot the size of a man's fist just below my sternum.

No, this isn't a heart attack. It's a panic attack.

I didn't know a panic attack could last five days until this one. Anxiety has been my faithful, though unpredictable, tormenter since I was 18 years old. I remember sliding down the wall in the hallway on a field trip, humiliated and afraid I might be dying. It's no less humiliating at thirty-five.

Anxiety takes all my hard work from the past six years and shreds it in an instant. And God, if You're actually listening and find Yourself thinking just how sad this sounds, that's because it is. When the three S's show up—silence, stigma, and shame—

it
shuts
me
down.

I don't think I can do this anymore!

I'm supposed to be a professional. An Amazon best-selling author. People know me as an in-demand speaker and life coach, a self-care consultant, and a recovery expert. All of those things are true, but when anxiety shows up, I feel needy and frail, like an infant. When it strikes, I feel incapable of caring for my own family or even myself.

One last thing, God—when my heart is overwhelmed, when anxiety paralyzes my mind, when a thousand tiny "maybes" and "should-haves" fill my thoughts, be my peace. Forget all those doubts I speak of so boldly as of late. Ignore the theological dissertations and questions that make me rage. What I could use right now is a friend that sticks closer than a brother. Please be bigger than the smoke and mirrors of man-made religion and show up for me today in the midst of this chaos. Come to me like calm and hold me while I quake.

Amen.

The journal entry you just read was the most overwhelmed I had felt since the day I nearly died by suicide. I almost didn't include this desperate prayer, for fear of scaring away potential readers with the rawness of such a confession.

But how can you write a book titled *Catching Your Breath* and not share the moments that knock the wind right out of you and leave you gasping? After all, I'm not alone in this. We've all had those moments. We've all had terrible days that left us wondering if stress and exhaustion will last forever.

The good news? They won't.

I think the reason I felt embarrassed once I regained control of my emotions that day was that I usually pride myself on the stories I craft. Maybe I haven't won a Pulitzer yet, but I have figured out how to tell a story. That particular week took all of my mindfulness and consideration and crafting and threw it out the window.

When life is tragic or just difficult, my inner chaos usually first presents as a stomachache. The day I wrote that journal entry, I thought I had a virus. It took me twenty-four hours to realize I was anxious, frustrated, and overwhelmed.

During this spiral, I missed two days of work because I felt like I was drowning. I vacillated between wanting to vomit, wondering if my gallbladder was inflamed, and blaming anxiety. After a few days, a couple of trusted friends helped me understand that beneath the tension was a current of anger. And not just any kind of anger—rage.

I'd recently had an opportunity that was so good I could hardly comprehend it. I desperately wanted to take it. However, after talking it over with my wife, Lindsey, we decided it wasn't the wisest decision. So I declined.

I didn't realize just how disappointed I would feel over the next few days. Turning down the opportunity was the right decision, but it wasn't easy. And that disappointment decided to manifest as rage.

Have you ever been baseball-bat-to-the-television angry? I've been there a handful of times in my life, but I had never learned how to connect and deal with the anger until I wrote this journal entry. I can easily empathize with others' emotions, but recognizing, processing, and verbalizing my own still requires a lot of work.

Rage scares me, so I've always internalized it. I grit my teeth, swallow the flames, and force that fire down into my belly. But anger always stems from something else that needs to be dealt with. And being visibly pissed off is perfectly acceptable when handled in a healthy way.

Once I was able to acknowledge and connect with my anger, you know what I did? I pulled over on the side of the road, texted my wife, and said, "I'm safe. But I'm going to be home a little late. I need to deal with this anger so that I can be my best self when I get home." Then I pulled back onto the highway and started to scream at the top of my lungs. It wasn't pretty. It wasn't controlled. It wasn't scripted. It was honestly pretty damn scary for someone used to avoiding anger. Thankfully, it was well after dark so nobody could see me completely losing my shit behind the steering wheel.

Hot tears ran down and soaked my shirt while I told God just how much the situation sucked. "Will my life always be this way? Will I always have to pass on great opportunities? Where is the grace? When do I get to move forward?! Do you even give a damn?! Could you just give me a break?!"

Through my years of ministry, recovery from a suicide attempt, and work as a life coach, I've learned one valuable, but sometimes sad, truth: I am not alone. Countless people are overwhelmed, suffering the shameful lashings of their past, holding onto gut-wrenching memories, unable to catch their breath in a world that tells them just to keep pushing. If the pressure of fear, pain, anxiety, and anger simmer and grow, sooner or later they're going to explode.

We have lost bright lights to this suffering. People like Robin Williams, Anthony Bourdain, Kate Spade, Chester Bennington, and even my friend Amy Bleuel, founder of Project Semicolon, have all succumbed to it. Despair is no respecter of persons. Mental illness doesn't give a damn about your pedigree or future plans. The treachery of hopelessness, the stigma of depression, and the harsh pain that lies to us, convincing us that suicide is the only answer; these things don't just rob us of celebrities and heroes. They killed my aunt and murdered a friend of mine when we were only children, leaving his twelve-year-old body hanging lifeless in his bedroom closet.

Despair is a literal killer. I wrote this book because so many people tend to just "fake it 'til you make it," but that is the worst thing we could possibly do. We don't have to shove the anger and disappointment back down into our gut. We don't have to pretend everything is okay while we're silently imploding. We can (and should) tell the truth, admit we're hurting, and ask for help.

People say time heals all wounds, but that isn't completely true. Sometimes, when we're going through a difficult time, we can't just keep moving. Just keep pressing through. Just keep slogging through the mud with all that weight on our backs. I love the movie *Finding Nemo*, but when it feels like we're drowning, we can't "just keep swimming."[2]

If we want to heal the deepest parts of our souls, it does take time, just like with any physical wound. But I know from years of personal experience that it also takes medication, therapy, self-compassion, stillness, a safe community, and willingness to take actionable steps to get better.

The world is full of overwhelmed people who are just trying to fake it till we make it. I wore the mask of performance and perfection for many years. But honesty and vulnerability have brought a new kind of strength, healing, and energy to my life. I don't ever want to go back. Maybe we can fake it till we make it, but it's a rotten way to live. And really, is it even living?

If it seems like more people are dying by suicide lately, it's because they are. The numbers are rising. The overwhelming sense of inner chaos leaves many feeling hopeless and alone. And diagnosed mental illness is a kind of life sentence no one would willingly choose.

I know, because I've been there.

I've been consumed with shame and bogged down by depression. I've been spun-up by anxiety and thrown into the damn wall by PTSD. I know what it's like to rest the Bible in my lap in a hotel room while writing "goodbye letters" to all my closest people.

When loneliness mixes with mental illness, shame, and a generalized sense of hopelessness, it's a cocktail that can destroy everything. Most importantly, it can ruin you. I know what it's like to think it would be better to die than to face tomorrow. I've walked through that living hell.

And I've faced tomorrow. And tomorrow isn't always more comfortable. The sun doesn't always come out right away. Things don't always miraculously change and improve overnight. Anyone who tells you just to do a particular something and suddenly life will make sense doesn't have a clue what on earth they're talking about.

Remember the scene in *Forrest Gump* where Forrest and Jenny are kneeling in the cornfield, praying, "Dear God, make me a bird so I can fly far, far away from here"?[3] I wish life worked that way. Like we could just rub Buddha's belly on the way out of the restaurant or throw a penny in a wishing well and suddenly get what we want. We wish God were some kind of celestial Santa Claus or the genie in Aladdin's lamp, just waiting to grant our every wish.

But God's not like that. Anyone who tells you otherwise is lying. And life just doesn't work that way. Don't let any televangelist or snake oil salesman deceive you. Life can be hard, uncertain, unfair, and unpredictable. But with the right resources, professional support, and self-care, the sun will come out eventually, or you'll learn to dance in the rain. Things do get better, bit by bit.

All we have is the present moment and each other. And we need each other! I need you to hold onto me just as much as you need me to tell you, "This will get better." This book is a call to treat ourselves and others with kindness, patience, presence, and compassion. Let's decide to show up and ask the difficult questions and tell the truth even when it feels like it will rip our beating hearts from our chests.

If you're reading this and it feels like life just plain sucks, I'm sorry. Please know you're not alone. It will get better. I promise. Please don't give up. Don't leave. This will get better. I don't know how or when. But if you are desperate to believe life won't always feel this way, this book can help. I know that hard days can seem unthinkable at times, but in my experience, they don't last forever.

So hold on. And let go of all the things that are weighing you down. If it feels like your ship is sinking, throw all the excess cargo overboard and hold on. Hold onto these words. Hold onto hope. Hold onto memories of better days. They will come again.

When the church or culture at large tells you to keep pushing, ignore your feelings, discount your needs, demonize your weaknesses, avoid your doubts, and *just keep swimming*, this is your invitation to come up for air and breathe again. This book is one big-ass permission slip: you can slow down and take a deep breath.

ON THE USE OF
RELIGIOUS LANGUAGE

I was born into a family that had been "wowed" by Jesus. Dr. Wayne Dyer wrote the book, *There's a Spiritual Solution to Every Problem*[4], but I think my folks would have written something like, *Jesus is the Solution to Every Problem*. In fact, I heard countless sermons on that exact theme. I believed it, too, until a suicide attempt in my late twenties forced me to start asking questions that didn't sit well with my church.

These days, I see many solutions to most problems and many avenues to Ultimate Truth. I see more questions than answers. My faith is more fluid than ever as I look for practical, actionable steps in the midst of chaos. It doesn't mean I don't pray or meditate or seek wisdom from the Bible—I do—but I heard a long time ago that "some people are so Heavenly-minded that they're of no earthly good," and it's true. I'm more interested in cultivating compassion and understanding in this life than I am about finding the quickest exit strategy to get to the "Pearly Gates" or whatever actually happens after we die.

If you find comfort in well-worn patterns of religious tradition, you are welcome here. And if you get lost in all the Christian jargon, you are welcome here, too. I've spent time in both of those camps. As a result, instead of offering you something like *Seven Simple Steps to Utopia*, I want to share practicality and a little hard-won wisdom I have gained along my journey.

There are several places in this book where I refer to deities like "God" and "Jesus." Please don't let it scare you away. If they don't fit your religious narrative or spiritual journey, that's okay. I believe that the Universe is big enough to handle our limited explanations. Those deities just happen to be the way I have most often experienced things like Divine Love, Hope,

Peace, and Joy. I'm a big fan of Gandhi, Buddha, and Mr. Rogers too. So try not to get tripped up on names and labels.

I've struggled with those labels, too. When it came to religion, it always seemed that if it's not perfect, it's worthless. I exhausted myself, attempting to live up to every unrealistic expectation of religious leaders and armchair theologians. So, for a while, I became an angry deconstructionist.

Maybe you've had a similar experience, stubbornly seeking the approval of the institutional church, but only becoming more disenfranchised and disillusioned. I get it. If you have more questions than answers, me too. I have been angry, frustrated, and worn out.

I've walked through six years of intense deconstruction of my own personal religious narrative, then reconstructing and moving forward. This is not a book about religion or even intertwined with specific religious ideology. Sure, we'll talk about spirituality here and there, but this is a book about overwhelmed people, desperate to find peace in the midst of chaos.

So this is a book for Christians? Sure. It's also a book for atheists, agnostics, Protestants, Catholics, non-religious Jews, mystics, blacks, whites, straights, gays, transgenders, and everyone in-between. In this book, I'm not here to argue sacred vs. secular or Sunday vs. Monday. I'm less concerned with a need for theological rightness and far more passionate about kindness. I'm here to encourage everyone who shows up, from all walks of life, to keep on keepin' on in the constant push and pull of a life that is rarely ever easy.

This is my invitation to you, whoever you are: *come and rest.* I encourage you to bring your exhaustion, doubts, frustrations, and disappointment. In the midst of a sometimes-chaotic life, it's normal to feel breathless. This book is the journey I've taken to cultivate calm. Join me in embracing authenticity, silencing your inner critic, calling out the lies you believe about yourself, and getting your life back. I pray (hope? cross my fingers?) that it is helpful and hopeful for you.

You're safe here.

Steve Austin

one

DROWNING

Who is he?
A railroad track toward hell?
Breaking like a stick of furniture?
The hope that suddenly overflows the cesspool?
The love that goes down the drain like spit?
The love that said forever, forever
and then runs you over like a truck?
Are you a prayer that floats into a radio advertisement?
Despair,
I don't like you very well.
You don't suit my clothes or my cigarettes.
Why do you locate here
as large as a tank,
aiming at one half of a lifetime?[5]

—Anne Sexton

When I was a little boy, my dad was my hero. One summer when I was 5 or 6, we took a trip to Nashville for a few days to visit my dad's best friend. The hotel had a pool. I distinctly remember standing on the stairs at the entrance to the shallow end when Dad said, "Okay, ready to count? Let's see how high you can count & how long I can stay under."

My dad, the career firefighter and marathon runner, held his breath and slipped beneath the surface of the water. I watched him swim away, toward the shallow end, turn, and slowly make his way back.

For the first few seconds, it was so cool, but to a kindergartener, staying under past the count of ten seemed either impossible or superhuman. He didn't come up for what felt like forever, and I was getting nervous. You know, 60 seconds seems like an eternity if you're a small child.

When my dad finally emerged and took that first gasp of fresh air, I was both relieved and amazed. I cheered, "Dad! Oh my gosh! I counted to 60! How did you do that?!"

As awed as I was to see my dad's trick, I always felt better when my hero was near me. The water was an uncertain thing to me: I knew I couldn't hold my breath and swim for it like he did. And I didn't like feeling alone.

It's interesting, children can't hold their breath as long as adults can. But the older we become, the longer we teach ourselves to hold it in. The same is true in life. Countless people are holding their breath and fears, just waiting to exhale.

A Case of the Mondays

You curse the alarm as it blares in your ears. The new baby was up on-and-off all night. So you were up, too. Your mother-in-law was staying in the guest room to "help," but she slept soundly all night long.

You have a flat tire because it's Monday morning and Mondays were made for flat tires. You think to yourself, "I cannot handle one more thing." You finally get on the road, knowing you're already ten minutes late for work, just to find cars backed up for miles. Of course, there's an overturned tractor-trailer on the interstate.

Your blood pressure spikes and anxiety grips your chest as you realize you can't afford to be late. There are rumors of layoffs at work and everyone wonders which staff meeting will be their last. You can't afford to give them a reason to sack you.

Maybe you slam a fist into the steering wheel and growl with frustration.

Or spill a cup of coffee down your shirt and have a total meltdown in the breakroom, leaving coworkers staring.

If I were there, I'd pull your coworker aside and whisper, "Trust me, friend: it's never about the spilled coffee."

Look, you don't need an official mental health diagnosis to have a meltdown. There are plenty of mostly normal people with relatively ordinary lives and good families who completely lose their shit in chaotic moments.

Can you blame them? At one point or another, we all know what it's like to fear an unpredictable future, dread an encounter with that overbearing person, or experience the shame of an unforgiving past. We stress out over people and situations that we cannot change or control. And then we beat ourselves up about it.

Why are we so hard on ourselves? When I make a mistake, I can be hateful, vile, and just plain mean to myself. Why do we do it? Sure, we mess up. No one is arguing that, but why do we treat ourselves worse than we'd treat our worst enemy? We're human, and for some reason, the Divine didn't program us for perfection. Therefore, there will be times we screw things up.

But instead of talking about the problem (we made a mistake), we view *ourselves* as the problem. Instead of calling it like it is and saying, "I messed up," we say, "I'm a loser."

What an idiot.
I'm so stupid.
I'm a mistake.
I am a failure.

We give ourselves no room for mercy. We accept no imperfections or flaws. Even if we might offer someone else a second chance, we refuse it for ourselves, condemning ourselves to a life sentence of self-hatred, criticism, and shame. And for what? Making a mistake? Being human? Dropping the ball?

Weak Sometimes

When my son, Ben, was around four years old, I took him with me to the grocery store. As I pushed the cart past the yogurt and cream cheese, I stopped to add a dozen eggs to my cart. I opened the carton and carefully inspected each one. I asked Ben if he knew what I was doing. "Checking to see if they're broken," he said. I was pleasantly surprised.

A few days later, I was reminded of those eggshells as I had lunch with a close friend. Kendra always seems to have it together, even in the face of heartbreak and adversity. Few people knew about her unfaithful husband who liked to spend grocery money on his drug habit. She loved him desperately but worried about being able to keep the lights on. She wondered whether Child Protective Services would find out and take her babies away.

Kendra took a second job to make ends meet and never asked a soul for help. While keeping up appearances is something we Southerners pride ourselves on (that and college football), she wasn't so concerned about what others thought. My friend was just doing what she could to be strong for her kids. She was just trying to make it another damn day.

I had watched Kendra walk through difficult decisions and unbearable circumstances with dignity and grace for years. She'd been pulled in every imaginable direction without friends, family, or coworkers realizing the hell she lived in.

Until she couldn't. Kendra had been one of the strongest people I knew, but as I sat across from her, I could see her sudden fragility. Years of chaos and mess had nearly broken her. I knew I needed to tread carefully.

I feared she had become like those eggshells, ready to crack at any moment. I wondered if her thin shell might crumble if I asked one more question.

Those moments aren't easy. When someone I care about seems to be suffocating underneath the weight of life, my deep-rooted habits flare up. My savior complex kicks into overdrive and I have to restrain myself from looking for the nearest phone booth to change from suit to superhero.

I love my friends, so it was tough not to try and swoop in as Kendra's guardian angel. Cherry-picked Christian scriptures that had been drilled into my head over the years flooded back, along with all the times I'd been told God would magically fix everything if we just pray hard enough. But I couldn't bear to use Bible verses to give a false sense of hope.

I wanted everything to be alright, and I wanted to play a part in it all working out. But I saw the sadness, exhaustion, and loneliness in my friend's eyes. Kendra wasn't looking for a Super Christian or a savior. She just needed space to breathe. She just needed me to embrace the tension of uncertainty with her and let her know that I saw her. This "got-it-to-gether, keep-it-together, don't-let-them-see-you-cry" friend of mine was trusting me with her pain and weariness and fear of all that felt uneasy.

It was a holy moment.

An eggshell holds it all together and protects everything inside. But one foul shake of the carton, one sharp drop, one little push, and *splat*, out spill baby chicken guts. The harsh reality is this: sometimes, even good eggs crack. In those moments, friends and loved ones get the chance to pad the carton with an extra layer of love. And at the end of the day, that's all we've got: uncertainty, hope, and the compassion of those who care about us.

In moments of personal despair, the Bible mostly either confuses me or pisses me off. Even as a pastor, sometimes the only part that seemed fully human to me was the Book of Psalms, a collection of songs, poems, confessions, and laments that people wrote in the best and worst moments of their lives. One portion that resonates deeply with me is this confession by King David (Psalm 142:4-6):

> *I'm up against it, with no exit—*
>   *bereft, left alone.*
> *I cry out, God, call out:*
>   *'You're my last chance, my only hope for life!'*
> *Oh listen, please listen;*
>   *I've never been this low.*

I'm certainly no Bible scholar, but it does seem that David understood what it was like to live in all sorts of chaos. King David was a royal screw up. His confessions in the Psalms are a roller coaster of emotions, but I think he had genuine faith. David's story is incredibly human and tragically flawed. He was a military veteran, had an affair, knocked up his baby's mama, and then had her husband killed. Can somebody say, "Jerry Springer episode?" Chapter by chapter, this trainwreck of a "man after God's own heart" famously flip-flopped from hope to fear, doubt to certainty, despair to peace, anger to sadness, chaos to calm.

As I write this, I'm listening to my very favorite, always-on-repeat song: "Weak Sometimes" by Devin Balram. Here's what it says:

> *You're put together, you're so well and put together*
> *That even on your tragic days, you seem fine*
> *You try so hard to hide that there's a fight inside*
> *But I can see it in your eyes that you're not fine*

Whoever said it was wrong to be weak sometimes
To cry yourself to sleep & wake up with your tears
  barely dry
You might feel like you're dying, that the end is nowhere
  near in sight
But whoever said it was wrong to be weak sometimes?

You say that pain just gets in the way
Just let it sit, it'll dissipate
You say that no one's had a better day
By dealing with their shame

Whoever said, it was wrong to be weak sometimes
To cry yourself to sleep & wake up with your tears
  barely dry
You might feel like you're dying, that the end is nowhere
  near in sight
Whoever said it was wrong to be weak sometimes?[6]

Damn, I love those words. After all, we're all weak sometimes. Or if we're not, it's just because we're so busy holding our breath and trying to "just keep swimming." Like my friend Mike said recently, "We're all doing one of the hardest things possible. *Living.*"

When I was much older than the little boy watching my dad from the shallow end, I was acutely aware of what it felt like to hold your breath so long that the pain and shame feel like drowning. For me, the end of the rope looked like waking up in an ICU hospital room after a serious suicide attempt. That was the point I started to learn how to breathe again.

Humaning Ain't Easy

In chapter five of the biblical book of John, Jesus was at a well-known spot for healing called the Pool of Bethesda. Legend had it that an angel would come stir up the water every so often and whoever got in first would be miraculously healed. So countless sick and disabled people hung around the water, watching and waiting for their chance to slip into the swirling waters.

One guy had been an invalid for thirty-eight years, but he hadn't received his healing because no one would pick him up and carry him to the water's edge when it began to churn. Jesus heard the man's story and said, "Get up. Take your mat with you, and walk!" And the man did.

What was different? The man didn't even have to step into the water. What changed? He didn't know it, but what he had actually been waiting on for nearly forty years was for someone to come along and say, "It's okay." He just needed permission.

What are you waiting for permission for?

Permission to do something.
Permission to quit something.
Permission to say something.
Permission to question.
Permission to rest.
Permission to cry.
Permission to not give a damn.
Permission to expect better.
Permission to still be upset.
Permission to move on.
Permission to seek a better way.
Permission to be weak.

Beneath all the different things we think we need permission for, I believe what we need is permission to be ourselves. Permission to belong, just as we are.

Mostly, I think we're all in desperate need of permission to be human.

Have you ever secretly wished you could tell someone what you really think? Not necessarily in that "I'mma give her a piece of my mind" kind of way, but just the ability, space, or courage to peel back the plastered smiles, stop hiding what you're feeling, and show everyone who you really are underneath? *Yeah. Me too.*

Instead, we allow rules of institutions, unrealistic expectations of others, outdated cultural norms, and our own toxic self-hatred to cake on our souls like Playdoh on my four-year-old's chubby palms. Grime, snot, and purple marker mix with sweat in her little hands as she unintentionally paints the glass of our beautiful French doors. Our spirits look similar, smeared with pain, performance, ego, and fear of what everyone else thinks.

Some days I have to stand in the bathroom, face set firm, staring in the mirror, giving myself permission to be human. Sometimes I still have to remind myself to untie the cape from my neck, come down off the cross, and take a deep breath.

You too? It's tough to stop. But, friend, do whatever it takes to snap back to this reality: you are human. You are only one person—only capable of doing so much before you completely forget about the fragile beauty of your being. You have permission to be yourself.

Because guess what? You're a freakin' human!

Not a robot or an algorithm or the newest AI technology. Not a spreadsheet or a superhero or the savior of the whole damn world. Your name is probably something like Cindy or Billy or Tom or Tammy or Steve or Jon. It's probably not Jesus (unless you're Latino) or Clark Kent or anyone else with a cross or a cape on their back.

Before you're ever part of any group or carry any label—be it Christian, Democrat, parent, spouse, teacher, student, or any ethnicity/nationality/gender/orientation—before ANY of that, you are a human.

We're human. That's it! And it's cause for celebration, and a call for radical grace. Humaning ain't easy (let's not even get started on adulting).

We are bruised, yet brave.
Once broken, now held together by strands of love,
Proudly on display on the front porch of God's house.

A tapestry of red and yellow, black and white,
Flapping in the breeze of the Holy Spirit.
Unashamed. Unafraid. No longer willing to hide.
Slaves no more.

Standing tall.
Fists on hips.
Courage
Just behind our ribs.

The man in John 5 had been an invalid: sick and unable to care for himself. Pronounced another way, the word means something entirely different. *In-valid*: not valid. Not legitimate. Not significant.

The sick man needed someone to validate him. To confirm him. To approve of him. He needed someone to tell him his life mattered. He was longing for meaning. Just like many of us, he needed permission to be human.

As Jesus spoke, I imagine the man heard something very different than simply, "Get up and walk." I think he heard something more like:

> *"You have believed your life doesn't matter for far too long. You have worth. In spite of your past, your imperfections, and what everyone else thinks about you, I am giving you permission to get up and walk away. Get up and leave this place. It is time to move on. Be different. Be new. Don't look back."*

Did you notice that Jesus didn't even address the man's issues? Jesus wasn't blind: I'm sure He noticed the guy's problems. But Jesus loved beyond the labels. He saw past the illness, to the heart of a human being who had been created by Divine Love. While others had tossed him a few coins to silence his cries, Jesus came along and embraced him in the fullness of his humanity. Jesus is always more concerned with wholeness than holiness.

Jesus recognized the man as a person and helped him find purpose in the midst of the struggle. In recovering his value, the man was able to see himself as an equal, probably for the first time in his life. And that may have been the greatest grace of all.

Whoever you are, whatever your story, whether you even believe in this spiritual stuff or not, listen to the invitation of Jesus, my favorite human:

> *"Come to me, all you misfits. Come and rest. Bring your story, covered in grit and grime and glitter and let's write something brand-new together. Come to me, all you who have been told you don't belong. Let Love create beauty from the ashes. Sit next to me, you who have believed you'll never be enough. There is space at the table for each of you who've grown weary from holding your breath for far too long.*

Come to me. Come and rest. You are welcome here, just as you are."

Even if you don't believe in Jesus, take those words as an invitation to exhale all the pain, anxiety, anger, and everything else you have been holding on to. We'll learn to breathe in calm and newness together. *We've got this!* The journey is all about learning to embrace the whole person, which requires cultivating mental, emotional, and even spiritual wellness.

I'm not a medical professional; I'm just a guy who survived a shipwreck and found the courage to talk about it. Much like the day my dad finally laid his head against the edge of the pool and drew a deep breath after his long stretch underwater, my journey from chaos to calm started after years of holding everything inside, blindly hoping all the pain and stress would magically disappear.

No matter how superhuman someone may seem, we all know what it's like to feel completely overwhelmed by life. We are all desperate for the safety of the shallow end. The good news? We don't have to live like this forever.

Welcome to the shallow end, friend.

GOOD NEWS FOR
SPIRITUAL MISFITS

*Faith comes and goes. It rises and falls
like the tides of an invisible ocean.*

Flannery O'Connor[7]

My little boy is a Lego maniac. He's six years old and his imagination astounds me. And his attention to detail *obviously* comes from his mother. Ben often goes to Build Night at the local Lego store with his grandma. He and other little architects follow along to create something new there. Sometimes, he brings home extra kits to build. My wife and I would guide him at first, but now he flies solo, piecing together characters, airplanes, and superheroes.

Ben got several new kits for Christmas. Details aren't my thing, but I adore that little boy, so I sat with him for some quality time as he worked. At first, things were going great. Ben followed the booklet and I watched the character take shape section by section, piece by piece. But the longer he worked, the more I noticed tension building between his excitement and his frustration. As good as he was, the intricate diagrams were a lot for a little fella.

Ben was about 80% complete when he started growling in anger. "Hang on, we've got this," I said. But he shocked me by smashing his brand-new toy to bits. There were tears and screaming and loads of disappointment.

He had realized he'd put one piece in wrong, several steps back. It couldn't have been any bigger than 2cm x 2cm, but that one, out-of-place Lego meant he couldn't fit the next piece in. It wasn't perfect and to my son, if it's not perfect, *it's worthless.*

Just like Ben's little out-of-place Lego piece, I've struggled with being a square peg in the round hole of orthodox religion. Growing up in the Bible Belt, life seemed fairly simple: you were either "sinner" or "saint," Christian or not. There were rules and expectations to follow, so I did. Until I couldn't follow them anymore.

What Now?

After being released from the psych ward, Lindsey drove the two hours, picked me up, and drove us home. I leaned my seat back and watched the green overpass signs on the interstate fly by. My life had fallen apart just one short week before. All I could wonder was, "What will tomorrow be like?" And "will I ever be able to go back to a church again?"

Up to this point, church had consumed my waking hours. I was steeped in the ways of Southern Evangelicalism all my life, then went to Bible college, and eventually served in some form of paid ministry for nearly 10 years. I knew the rules: when to stand, sit, kneel, and raise my hands. Still, all the external *doing* of orthodox Christianity wasn't enough to save me. I could read church people like a book, and I knew how to play the game. But I was dying inside. I nearly died on the outside, too.

I knew that if I was going to move forward and get my life back, everything would have to change. This included the ways I connected with the Divine. These days, I'm not so sure about all the rules and expectations. And that is the biggest part of my faith struggle. My walking-away-from-everything-I-was-raised-on-into-the-vast-unknown struggle. For the past few years, my biggest frustration when it comes to Christianity has been this: I live in the in-between. I am the Lego piece that doesn't fit.

Christian Agnostic

"Agnostic" is a word that freaks out a lot of fundamental Christians. People don't like "agnostic" for many of the same reasons no one ever votes for an Independent—we don't know what to do with people who choose to no longer toe the party line. But I love this definition: *a person who holds neither of two opposing positions on a topic.*[8]

In the opening of *Agnostic*, Lesley Hazleton says this:

> *To be agnostic is to love this kind of paradox. Not to skirt it, nor merely to tolerate it, but to actively revel in it. The agnostic stance defies artificial straight lines such as that drawn between belief and unbelief. It is free-spirited, thoughtful, and independent—not at all the wishy-washy I-don't-knowness that atheists often accuse it of being.*

Hazelton continues:

> *What's been missing is a strong, sophisticated agnosticism that does not simply avoid thinking about the issues, nor sit back with a helpless shrug, but actively explores the paradoxes and possibilities inherent in the vast and varied universe of faith-belief-meaning-mystery-existence. That's my purpose here.*
>
> *I want to explore unanswerable questions with an open mind instead of approaching them with dismissive derision*

> *or with the solemn piety of timid steps and bowed head—to get beyond old, worn-out categories and establish an agnostic stance of intellectual and emotional integrity, fully engaged with this strange yet absorbing business of existence in the world.*[9]

Me too, Lesley. Yes, I still hold the example of the Jesus of the Bible at the center of my life, but I am finally admitting I have more questions than certainty, more doubt that belief, more possibilities than answers. I'm not sure folks like me are welcome any longer in the most fundamental corners of the Evangelical church. When it comes to dualistic thinking, my *but* always gets in the way. I don't buy the message that you are either good or bad, black or white, right or wrong, sacred or profane. Religion sees life through the lens of duality: this or that.

Things of orthodoxy and Christian theology just don't always make sense or line up exactly right for me. So these days, I'm wearing the label of "Christian Agnostic," as a badge of honor. I supplement my spiritual journey with principles from countless other traditions, and I'm perfectly comfortable with the following three words: *I don't know.*

Giving Up My Thrift Shop Faith

My wife and I love to shop at garage sales and thrift stores. We both grew up going to them, so giving new purpose to old pieces of furniture is a fun challenge for two Millennials with more student loan debt than a show dog could jump over.

Our kitchen table is a wooden corner booth that originated either in a camper or a houseboat. I'm guessing it's from the 60's. It's small and has little water marks and pencil indentations on the top—proof that it once belonged to someone else, but we love it. "It's got character," Lindsey tells me.

Recycling and repurposing is one of the things we do best. The only thing I don't really like to buy from our thrift shop is clothing. There's no dressing room, and it's a real inconvenience to have to take it home, see if it fits, and if it doesn't, return the item for an exchange.

And the only thing worse than recycled clothes is secondhand, thrift shop faith.

When it comes to Evangelical Christianity, I've pretty much done it all. I was basically born in the baptismal. Sang my first solo at 5. Children's camp. Youth leader. Ministry school. Youth pastor. Worship pastor. Church, church, church. Jesus, Jesus, Jesus. And I believed it all.

Still, for all those years, I was only repurposing the faith of my parents and grandparents. I brought home a thrift shop faith assembled from bits and pieces I acquired over time. I guess that's true for most of us. But for too long, it seemed like too much trouble to return what didn't fit and find something better. So I held on to traditions and expectations that weren't mine for thirty years. They weren't necessarily wrong ideas, they just didn't fit me because they belonged to someone else. I was terrified to stop recycling those things and trying to squeeze myself into them. But when something just doesn't fit, no amount of dressing it up will do.

I wish I could just accept things with "faith" and "because the Bible says so." But that just doesn't cut it for me anymore. I'm not even talking about some of the crazier ideas, like "speaking in tongues" or being "slain in the Spirit." I have big questions and doubts, questions like:

- Did the resurrection of Jesus actually happen?
- Is Hell a real, geographical place?
- Is original sin accurate? Or are we divine from birth?

- Is Jesus really the only way to God? And if not, *what are we even doing here, in church, week after week?*

For the last year of my long five-year process of deconstruction, I had to re-examine everything that marked my life for the first thirty years. It was more than stressful. It was excruciating. I thought that, because I couldn't seem to shove my not-so-sure-faith into the tiny box of toxic, fear-based religion, I just couldn't be a Christian. Surely there was no place for me at God's table. And if I couldn't be just like everyone else, shove my faith into that box, shut the hell up and follow the damn rules, then I didn't belong. So I quit for a while.

But eventually, I gave myself the grace to start again and find a better way. I began to cultivate genuine faith in the uncertainty. I was surprised to find Jesus still at the center of my faith journey. But I was thrilled to learn everyday spirituality comes with lots of choices.

Everyday Spirituality

Everyday spirituality is connecting the head and the heart in a way that works for *you*. It's not about doctrine, dogma, or doing the right things. It's acknowledging that, in order for you to be a healthy, whole person, you need to find what restores your head and heart and then do that every single day.

It's about something deeper than Sunday morning Christianity. While that works really well for some people, you may need more. You may need something different. Everyday spirituality is about relating to the Divine in a way that feels comfortable, like holey jeans, flip flops, and your favorite, faded t-shirt. (Unless you feel more comfortable in a three-piece suit and shiny shoes.) Everyday spirituality is about connecting with "Love made tangible" (as my friend Ed Bacon puts it), no matter where you are on the journey.

Everyday spirituality acknowledges at least these three things:

1. Man-made rules aren't for everyone.
2. Whatever has been crushed can be restored.
3. Everyone belongs, but not everything fits.

In being true to myself, I know that if I feel pushed into a corner the-ologically, with no flexibility, no choices, and only rigid religion, I will die. Man-made rules don't work for me. When I had depression so bad I couldn't find my smile even on sunny days, Divine Love showed up in the midst of the worst shitstorm of my life. And Grace allowed my crushed life to be restored. I never walked away from Jesus, just the rigid brand of religion that does more to exclude than make room. And I have no regrets.

As I continue to step further away from the religious machine, I am being drawn closer to the story of Jesus. These days, I am finding the grace of God by acknowledging that each person has their own heavy load to carry. And I am showing up to fulfill the call of Christ to help carry those burdens, as I am able. Whether it's behind the pulpit or in the pew next to me, I am choosing to embrace humanity rather than demonize it and finding that it makes me much better at this thing called Christianity.

When I feel that God is far away, unreachable, unclear, or hiding, all I need to do is connect with my neighbor. Red and yellow, black and white, straight, trans, Jew, Muslim, atheist, and every other varied color of the rainbow: together, each of you helps my picture of God come into focus.

Everyday spirituality is an invitation to open rather than close, to bloom rather than wilt, to listen rather than speak, to learn rather than attempt to convert.

Identifying as a spiritual misfit feels like *knowing* that everything is going to be all right in the end. It is this confident hope that Love is the Source of everything, even if I can't intellectually prove, explain, or even fully understand it. The freedom of identifying as a Christian Agnostic means I am finally ok with what I do not know.

Millennials and the Church

While being a Christian Agnostic feels lonely, my experiences are pretty typical of members of my generation raised in the Evangelical church. While older church leaders bemoan Millennials leaving the church, they reinforce the exact reasons why so many of us have left the faith traditions of our childhoods.

While many have walked away entirely in search of a better fit, some of us haven't completely given up on Christianity. We're convinced that Jesus was serious when he said, "Love one another." But much of what we've witnessed from institutions that operate in the name of God is pain and abuse. We feel like everyone in the church has a hidden agenda to try to "save" us, but we don't need to be saved, at least not in the way *they* think we do. We were once baptized by well-meaning people in fear, shame, and guilt. But we aren't buying that any more. We are coming up from those muddied waters, looking for new life.

When I woke up in an ICU room and decided I would keep living, I knew things had to change. And one of the biggest changes was getting rid of the things, theologies, and unrealistic expectations that were killing me. Moving forward meant letting go and choosing to accept myself, *just as I am*. Accepting *myself* allowed Perfect Love to do its work of casting out the fear that was entrenched in my heart, mind, and soul.

This is the new leg of my spiritual journey. I don't have it all figured out. And it's okay that you don't, either. If you disagree and you're still clinging to the black and white thinking of dualism, that's okay. You're safe here, too. I won't try to convert you and I hope to God you won't try to change me. (Insert smiley face emoji here.) I hope you find peace for your own journey, wherever you are. I may not have the certainty I once idolized, but I do have this calm *knowing* in my gut that Love is actually present with me, even when I'm not sure what I believe anymore.

Everyday spirituality carries a desperation for honesty. There's a hunger for conversation and celebration of diversity. In this stripped-down connection with our true selves, we can show up with our success, failure, vulnerability, questions, and what's left of our deconstructed faith.

We are shifting away from and sifting through the excesses of man-made religious constructs. These little Sunday School kids have grown up and read the Bible for ourselves. And we've read other stuff, too. We aren't afraid to learn from science and other religions. We are catching up with reality and culture while still embracing whatever faith means to us. We refuse to check our brains, political convictions, and common decency at the door.

Yes, we can respect the faith journey of previous generations, but we're carving our own path. And for those of us who still claim to be Christians, we are passionate about the overarching theme of the life and lessons of Jesus: love comes with no strings attached.

This is Good

I transitioned out of deconstruction and started rebuilding my spirituality at the beginning of 2018. That New Year's weekend, I sat on the back porch of the beach house we rented, whiskey on the rocks in one hand and a favorite stogie in the other. Every two to three minutes, I took a deep, slow breath and exhaled with a relaxed sort of hum.

I didn't notice my own sighs at first because I was so caught up in the moment, but as I did, I felt the stress and tension melt from my shoulders. It was like my whole body exhaled, not just my lungs. I imagine it felt something like the Biblical account of the creation story, where God completes the work and says, "this is good." *Maybe God had whiskey in one hand, too.*

The next morning, the wind blew through the palms while light rain danced on the roof of our beachside bungalow. The plink-a-tink-patter of raindrops against the tin made a wonderfully unpredictable rhythm of rest and repeat. With this heavenly symphony as my soundtrack, I couldn't help but consider the sound of a sigh.

Breath itself has no noise; it's the hum—the vibration of my voice box, the reverberation of my contented soul—that goes up past my heart and out my mouth to say, "This is good." I guess breath is a lot like wind—it isn't noticed until it brushes past your lips or tickles the sea oats. I would never have known the breeze was there until it played peek-a-boo around the neighbor's shutters. It whistled through the shingles, kissing the picnic table and lapping against the rocking chairs on the back porch. *This is good.*

I stood barefoot in the cold December sand, two days before New Year's, watching the waves wash over my feet, playing their tireless melody, inviting my soul to sigh again. *And sigh, it did.* The water swept in and out, brushing sand over my toes and quickly pulling it back again. The ocean inhaling and exhaling, whispering over creation, *this is good.*

It might sound too mystical or New Agey for most Christians. It might sound too Jesus-y for those who don't connect with Christianity. But that cold weekend, as one year ended and another began, God was doing a work of rest and restoration in my soul, beyond anything I may ever be able to comprehend or explain fully with words. And isn't that how it is with a deeply transformative experience? We can't ever seem to fully explain it to someone else, we just know we've been forever altered.

Even in my doubt, God kept impressing on me the universality of rest and repeat, rhythm and rhyme, start and stop. Like my friend Sue (to whom this book is dedicated) often reminds me: the world has an axis and I don't have to do anything to keep it spinning. "The merry-go-round has a motor," Sue says. "All you have to do is get on it and ride."

This weekend retreat was right after my freefall of deconstruction and I was *desperate* to find God again. Yes, there were doubts, loads of uncertainty, and the stretching tension of all I couldn't explain or understand; but in my soul, there remained a longing for something—or Someone—more.

And something—or Someone—met me. It's like God just wrapped my entire essence up in my grandma's quilt and said, "I'm right here. You don't have to do a damn thing to find me or catch my attention. Be still. Let's just breathe together. Listen to how I do it."

It was like the words of Jesus (Matthew 11:28-30, MSG) became tangible to me that day:

> *Are you tired? Worn out? Burned out on religion? Come to me. Get away with me and you'll recover your life. I'll show you how to take a real rest. Walk with me and work with me—watch how I do it. Learn the unforced rhythms of grace. I won't lay anything heavy or ill-fitting on you. Keep company with me and you'll learn to live freely and lightly.*

So I listened, to the in and out of the tides, the up and down of the waves, the inhale and exhale of my breath, the open and shut of the very valves of my heart. I couldn't get away from the rhythm of everything around me. The waves, the rain on the roof, the wind through the palms, the breath in my lungs, my heartbeat, the rocking chair—literally everything had a rhythm. Stop and go, rest and repeat. At a molecular level, all the energy of the earth was vibrating. It was singing praises to God, reminding me to join in: *rest and repeat.*

Just like all the weather and rhythm and creation didn't entirely make sense to me, I may never find the words to make it make sense to you. I don't totally understand it in my head. But in the deepest part of me, in the place past reason and logic and the religion of my childhood, something shifted. I was freed from my obsession with certainty. Instead, I was able to start saying, "It just is," and accept that. And I am accepted by the All that "just is."

This is what everyday spirituality is all about for me. This is good news for spiritual misfits. It's about not having all the answers, but accepting myself as I am. It's about journeying towards calm and wholeness, knowing God (or the universe, or my own soul) is moving with me, in me, and through me, every step of the way. *This is really good.*

NEKKID

I no longer look for the good in people, I search for the real...Because while good is often dressed in fake clothing, real is naked and proud no matter the scars.[10]

—Chrishala Lishomwa

I didn't talk to someone I love for nearly a year. We were never really best friends, but it still broke my heart to lose this lifelong relationship. The details of what transpired aren't nearly as important as the fact that simmers just beneath the surface: vulnerability is scary shit. We both wounded each other. We were angry and scared and hid behind a tough facade, pushing vulnerability away like a side of cold Brussel sprouts.

So many of us do this. Whether we've received explicit messages like "dry it up" or "showing emotion is weakness," or picked up more subtle signals from culture, we've all learned to fear vulnerability. It's difficult, exposing, and can make us feel defenseless and naked. But it's a crucial step on the journey toward calm.

The lie of modern American culture is this: don't get naked.

Have sex.
Watch porn.
Get freaky.

But don't get naked.

The path from chaos to calm begins with honesty. They say the truth will set you free, but it might make you extremely uncomfortable in the process. It strips away all the layers of cultural norms, religious expectation, family secrets, and perfectionism. *Do it anyway.* Once you start owning your story, no one can take it away from you. No amount of gossip or slander or disengagement can diminish the fact that you are not who you once were. Not giving up in the face of adversity will change you.

Brené Brown says it like this:

> When we deny our stories, they define us. When we own our stories, we get to write a brave new ending. I know this is true. I may have learned it as a researcher but I live this truth as a daughter, a partner, a leader, a sister, a mother, and a friend. When we push down hurt or pretend that struggle doesn't exist, the hurt and struggle own us.[11]

It's Okay to Get Nekkid

At the age of ten, I was a chubby, prepubescent blob of nerves. You can imagine just how horrified I was when my Grandpa took me to the YMCA one terrible morning. We walked into the locker room and I was appalled to realize it must have been Senior Citizen Saturday at the Y. Everything had lost its elasticity. Body parts were sagging below other body parts. The room was filled with white-haired old men that looked sort of like whole chickens, vacuum-sealed in the refrigerated section of the grocery store.

But those old men weren't just naked. They were *nekkid.* (Okay, it's the Southern pronunciation of the same word, but this is my book, so I'll write it how I want.) What is it with old people? They are either more confident than ever, or they've spent a lifetime caring about what everyone else thinks and they're just done. *Set the boys free, Gramps.*

Truth is, that Saturday wasn't terrible because these men were strutting around in all their saggy glory. It was because *I* was petrified of anyone seeing me without clothes on. I found comfort in a hoodie, even on warm days in Alabama. I preferred to wear a t-shirt at the pool because I didn't have the muscle tone of more athletic boys my age. So I did the mature, brave thing: I tied a towel around my waist and performed the most awkward, shimmying dance to change from street clothes to swimsuit without showing my most vulnerable parts.

My issues with my body and others makes sense when you consider the sexual abuse I endured as a preschooler. My wounds taught me the danger of vulnerability. Growing up in the sometimes-toxic 90's Evangelical purity culture only reinforced that nothing about my body was good. Girls were taught that sexuality and the female body was evil ("keep everything covered up or you'll make your brothers in Christ sin"). And we were all taught (either directly or indirectly) that even attraction to another person was bad. We'd better kiss dating goodbye (and kiss nothing else) if we knew what was good for us. During my years in Bible school, we had a purity ceremony, where we were "married to Jesus," and received a ring—yes, even the guys. (Because Jesus is the lover of my soul, *duh*.)

I'm much older than the little boy in the locker room with my granddad, but I still don't like to get nekkid. As uncomfortable and scary as it can be, I'm convinced that everyone needs to do it. Vulnerability empowers us to own our stories. Stripping away the facade and getting gut-level honest about who we are and where we've been isn't easy.

Nothing worth doing is easy. Plenty of people I know wouldn't be comfortable viewing their own bare forms in the mirror. No one starts out celebrating their scars, the extra weight around the middle, or that funny-shaped birthmark. Still, we all want the freedom of vulnerability, to be nekkid and unashamed, even if we don't know it yet. Doubt may shiver down our spines when we start to pull off our shirts. But we must learn to embrace ourselves if we are ever going to encourage others to do the same.

Saying Sorry

In the middle of writing this book, I received a two-page, handwritten letter from the loved one I hadn't spoken to in a year. In essence, he opened up to me and said what we all long to hear when we've been wounded: "I am so sorry." The sad reality is that I was honestly okay with writing him off, but he found the courage to be seen: to be naked and to reconnect. I'm not proud of my initial response, but this is a chapter on vulnerability, so hey, you get the whole story. My loved one's willingness to value our relationship over his own incredible discomfort taught me, once again, that anything that's been crushed can be restored. I'm forever grateful for this lesson and for the relationship we've been rebuilding since that day.

Part of living honestly is being willing to apologize. Are we willing to be honest about our mistakes, apologize and move forward? Are we ready to stop playing the blame game, start owning our stories and creating our futures?

Just like pebbles dropped in a pond, our actions ripple out and impact those around us. Even if there is no direct impact on the ones we love, the boldness and self-compassion we cultivate each time we share our stories allow us to fight fear, shame, and guilt better than ever before. Instead of unintentionally poisoning the relationships we most care about, we begin to strengthen the ties that bind us.

When we choose to become vulnerable, it is because something inside longs to be courageous, to tell the truth, and to speak the hard-won wisdom. It's the soul that begs us to tell a better story, one more in line with the truth of our being. We are no longer bound by what the past says about us and our best efforts to keep it hidden. We aren't trapped by the shameful lies that work so hard to hold us back from the best life has to offer. We are so much more than the residue of a terrible moment.

In the richness of our relationships, we discover a full life. Connection happens on the sacred journey toward wholeness. It shows up bit by bit as we build deeper trust with people we cherish. Regularly practicing vulnerability with your inner circle is vital. Maybe it's a weekly brunch with your best friend, confession with your priest, or a video chat with your sister who lives out of state. It doesn't matter how it looks: getting nekkid keeps us open and helps our hearts stay soft and warm. The coldness of everyday life and the demands of work and family can harden us quickly; regular doses of genuine connection is the perfect medicine for weary souls.

In a recent conversation, my friend Laura said, "Wouldn't it be incredible if, just for a moment, we could all see everyone's thoughts and secrets? Can you imagine how that would help us understand the person better?" What if we could see the abuse they've endured, the shame they were raised under, the pain they've experienced? What if we could see the good intentions behind their awkward words? Wouldn't it make us all more compassionate in our responses if we saw, just for a few grace-filled moments, how alike we are inside?

Anne Lamott said:

> We begin to find and become ourselves when we notice how we are already found, already truly, entirely, wildly, messily, marvelously, who we were born to be.[12]

When Naked is Uncomfortable

It's awkward when a total stranger shucks down in front of us, blinding us with emotional nudity. That's not what I'm advocating. It's usually not healthy to overshare with people we don't know. But these days, in appropriate settings with my inner-circle people, my goal is to take it all off. Vulnerability is now a big part of how I serve others, so I had to find the courage to get honest with myself first.

While I don't like being the naked grandpa, the first to strip down, it can make a profound difference. Whenever I go first in vulnerability, sharing even the raw parts of my story, I connect with others. That's true for all of us. When others are doing their best to keep things covered with that awkward towel dance, we can empower them to live honestly. We just need to share our own balance of courageous vulnerability and a gracious invitation to tell the truth.

For the first 28 years of my life, I was scared to death of being seen. My whole life was an awkward towel dance, trying to misdirect attention from the parts I wanted to keep hidden. At the time of my suicide attempt, I thought that if people realized who I was underneath all the layers of performance and people pleasing, they wouldn't accept me.

Does that sound familiar?

After a few months of individual therapy and marriage counseling, I learned that fear and shame are kissing cousins. They're always doing their damnedest to keep our pasts under lock and key and our futures as dim and predictable as possible. My wife promised to neither leave nor think less of me for opening the Pandora's box of my life and laying all my pain, secrets, fears, and shame out in the open. That gave me permission to stop performing and just be a human in need of love, honesty, and a second chance.

I remember the dark days of hiding my truth from the world. It nearly killed me. I buried secrets, pain, fears, and illnesses down deep, praying no one would ever find the real me. Spending a week on a psych ward after my suicide attempt wasn't my first choice: I was humiliated, defenseless, and scared. I could no longer run from the things I'd always hated about myself, and facing them was the last thing I wanted. But it was a huge step toward learning to own my story and get my life back.

I hope you don't feel that desperate before you find the courage to own your truth. I can't encourage you enough to get quiet and plumb the depths of your soul. It might be scary. You might feel defenseless. But give yourself permission to discover and embrace the truth of your being.

Who are you? Isn't that the question you've been asking all your life? Beyond your race, denomination, political convictions, or even your reputation—who are you? Below the noise and distractions, underneath the busyness and expectations—who are you?

What's your story? Is it your first memory? Maybe the hardest lesson you've ever learned? Or your most embarrassing moment? Your biggest screw-up? We've all got a story. Some of us are more comfortable sharing than others.

Self-discovery is the first step in getting your life back. It's time to get honest about who you are. What do you want? And what has been holding you back? If you're not ready to answer that question yet, stick with me. We'll get there together, but first, we've got to take you from chaos to calm.

The most courageous thing you can do on that journey is harness your inner grandpa, get nekkid, and let it all hang out.

FULLY KNOWN, FULLY LOVED

I shall know you, secrets
by the litter you have left
and by your bloody footprints.[13]

—Lola Ridge, 1873

We all have things nobody in the world knows about us. I know I still do. Often, the secret isn't the important part. Keeping it is. My problem is that I've never been good at keeping secrets.

On Friday, October 13, 2006, I finally paid off the beautiful wedding set that included a repurposed diamond from my grandmother's engagement ring. I called Lindsey's mom and stepdad to tell them my secret plan to propose at Thanksgiving. I texted photos of the ring and we schemed up details for my grand proposal.

Our scheming was fun, but it didn't last. The ring burned a hole in my pocket in a matter of hours and my heart was bursting with excitement. I couldn't possibly hold on for another six weeks. Before the end of night, I was on one knee on the patio of a Chinese restaurant. "I love you. Will you marry me?" was printed on a tiny slip of white paper tucked inside her fortune cookie.

I told you, I've never been good at keeping secrets.

What I should probably say is, I've never been good at keeping *happy* secrets. But secrets I've been ashamed of? No problem. In fact, one of the most difficult parts of married life for me was a nagging secret I'd held onto for years.

The secret I'd been holding onto for more than a decade was eating me alive. I was terrified to tell Lindsey. How could I *possibly* confess that one piece of my story? But moving from chaos to calm requires letting other people in, just like we learned in the prior chapter.

Sure, we can learn to be vulnerable with our hopes, dreams, and even the mundane ups and downs of daily life. But secrets are different...or at least they feel that way. If you have one big secret, like I did, it is likely the source of your most significant fear: *how can I be thoroughly loved if I am fully known?*

For years, I could not bring myself to tell the truth and live into my true identity. I had addictions and secrets and curiosities and a history of abuse and night terrors that I couldn't possibly tell anyone. I thought the only way to be loved and accepted was to hide everything, including my crippling depression and anxiety.

I couldn't bear to disappoint one more person, so I learned the song and dance everyone else was doing, and I did it perfectly. I knew the words to say and could quote Scriptures like all my friends, but my inner castle was built on the shifting sand of other people's opinions and approval. I was so accustomed to performing for others that I didn't even really know who I was. I just knew I wasn't the person everyone thought. And I was growing more exhausted with every passing day.

My secret became the most profound contributor to my shame. It started when I was just a boy and continued to build right up until the night I nearly died by suicide. I heard the call of Jesus to "come and rest" all my life, but I was nearly thirty years old, lying in an ICU hospital room, before I realized Jesus was serious. I had permission to be human. To admit

I was weak. To ask for help. To allow the power of confession to wash over my soul.

Apparently, I am better at keeping secrets than I realized. But just like the diamond ring in my pocket that crisp October evening, my secret managed to burn a hole in my soul. It always felt like such a toxic story, oozing poison, burying itself deeper into my psyche. It seems that secrets either kill us or resurrect us.

What about you? I bet you probably have at least one minor indiscretion from your past you'd rather not talk about. Who isn't ashamed of their scars and secrets? Does stigma keep you silent? Do you fear being caught in your addiction? Or shunned if they find out who you love?

What if your church friends found out that you have more doubt than faith these days? How would your tribe respond if you told them you don't vote like they do? What if your family found out about the affair, the eating disorder, or the child that isn't really his? Secrets come in all shapes and sizes.

We're all trying our best to make it on this great big ball of water, air, dust, heartache, loneliness, and joy. And most of us, sadly, are listening to the lies that tell us to keep our mouths shut and our heads down. We've honed the fine art of flying under the radar, but are miserable as hell. We try not to rock the boat, offend our families, or embarrass our partners, but we're drowning beneath the weight of an illusion. These lies are massive stones tied around our necks, pulling us to the ocean's floor as we gasp and clamor, desperate for air.

But the most dangerous lie about secrets is that we are alone and no one gives a damn about our story. When we believe this lie, we rob the world of our unique perspective on survival and success. If you believe your story doesn't matter, you're all alone on your tiny island of insignificance, and hold all those secrets inside until you die, you have kept your one great gift from the rest of us. No, the gift isn't your secret. It's allowing those who care about you to know you completely. *Fully known, fully loved.*

We've all got secrets and stories. We are bound together in an indescribable web of love and loss, triumph and failure. We are not alone, no matter our experiences, mistakes, and wounds. All those ups and downs mix with the beauty and tragedy of daily life, but the one thing that connects us all is the power of story.

Your story.

My story.

The human story.

The big difference between secrets and stories is whether or not we find the courage to share ours with others. If we hold all our experiences inside, fearful that others will trample our traumas and not validate our victories, the stone around our neck continues to grow. The longer we refuse to tell our truth, the deeper those secrets drag us. Secrets threaten to destroy, but all we have to do to defeat a secret is to speak it.

When you hold a story that no one else knows for your whole life, it eventually begins to call to you. At night, it beckons. In the morning, it whispers. In the sunshine or the rain, it makes its presence known. In the middle of a crowd or in the calm solitude, your secret is always there. It knows you, and if you're anything like me, your secret has been begging to be told.

After years of marriage and two children, Lindsey and I have grown closer than ever. Counseling worked. Reading the work of people like Brené Brown, Ed Bacon, and Paul Young has transformed us. One night after the kids went to bed, we watched a romantic movie, had a couple of drinks, some honest conversation, and ended the evening with some romance of our own.

When I awoke the next morning, I felt more connected to her than I had felt in a long while. I felt a rekindled affection that we didn't regularly experience in the ho-hum busyness of full-time work and parenting. In the past, I let this deep connection wash over me, but soon after, my secret would show up, whispering to me that I'm a fraud. It told me if I let her in, she would never get close to me again.

This particular morning, however, while she rubbed my back before I even opened my eyes, I knew it was now or never. In the warmth and closeness of her touch, as her toes ran down the back of my calves, I found more courage to speak my truth.

In the stillness of the morning, my heart pounded and nausea gripped me. But I remembered all the versions of me she had chosen to love so far. When I was a broke college kid, she loved me eagerly. I was a know-it-all Christian, and she loved me patiently. Through every mistake, misstep, and failure, she loved me mercifully. She loved me wholeheartedly, without condition. I had to take the risk that she would love me still.

That morning, we sat on the back porch in the cool of the morning. As rain pitter-pattered against the patio blocks, our conversation wound its way back to the sex from the night before, and we both blushed a little at just how much we enjoyed ourselves. I became emboldened because I saw the way she truly desired me, in spite of all she already knew about me. It was time.

I took the risk, and the power of confession took our relationship even deeper than I had hoped or imagined. My nervousness and shame almost seem laughable now. Why was I so afraid of being completely honest with this woman who nursed me back from death? Lindsey has proven her relentless love for me, time and time again, even at my darkest moments.

When my confession was over, we embraced and Lindsey planted the softest kisses on my neck. I felt wholly emptied, in the best way possible. She didn't shrink back in fear. She didn't pull away in disgust. She didn't confirm any of the irrational fears shame planted in my brain.

In his relationship workbook, *Five Dates*, Mike Foster says, "...loneliness does not come from being alone, but from being unheard."[14] Learning to truly hear and be heard by one another is a transformative, healing experience. Sometimes it takes counseling and lots of good books to get there. Sometimes it takes practice, telling our "smaller" secrets as we build the courage to tackle our big ones.

These days, I'm learning to ignore the voice of shame more often. It's easier to open up and own my truth now that Lindsey knows about it. Telling secrets works like that. We don't need to tell everyone everything about us. That's not healthy or helpful. But, by starting with the safest, most trustworthy people in our lives, we can slowly turn our secrets into stories that free us and those around us.

Author's note: Sometimes you don't feel quite ready to share your secret with your best friend or your partner. That's okay, too. In that case, it may be time to hire a professional. Pay an unbiased third party like a counselor, therapist, or life coach. Don't have the money? There are several clinics that work on a sliding scale, based on your income. You could also call the crisis line to get that heaviness off your chest. The Suicide Prevention Lifeline can be reached 24/7 at 1-800-273-8255.

WHEN YOU BELIEVE YOU ARE BAD

Please call me by my true names,
so I can hear all my cries and laughter at once,
so I can see that my joy and pain are one.
Please call me by my true names,
so I can wake up
and the door of my heart
could be left open,
the door of compassion.

—Thich Nhat Hanh[15]

Ryan wasn't out when we were in Bible college together. I'm sure people had their suspicions, but he never told anyone he was gay until years after he was expelled. While they officially dismissed him for smoking, I've always wondered if it had more to do with their suspicions about his sexuality. So did Ryan.

That experience turned Ryan's world upside-down. My friend was filled with shame and pain. From his perspective, his dream of working for a church was forever crushed. If our little Bible college didn't want him, how could God possibly love him? Heartache and anger were his constant companions as he internalized the rejection. He believed he was intrinsically bad, so he partied to numb himself. Alcohol, drugs, and wild living became his coping mechanisms.

We have remained friends through the years, and I've been privileged to hear more of his story. Once, I asked Ryan why his life got so rough after

Bible college. He said something I won't ever forget: "When you believe you are bad, you don't act good."

Ryan was desperate to accept and love himself as a gay man, to believe that God could love him in all of his gayness. He wanted to think that he was created with purpose and that there was room for him at God's table, too, but decades of toxic theology told him otherwise.

Of course, Ryan's not the only one. I've had similar, heartbreaking conversations with several dear friends. Through their tears, each confessed that trying to "act straight" was like living in a prison of secrecy and fear. These aren't just kids; they are adults who are scared to death of being disowned by their families and ostracized by their churches and communities.

The fears aren't unfounded. We've all heard horror stories about someone coming out and experiencing rejection, being shunned, and sometimes enduring outright violence, simply for being real about who they are. Is it any wonder people struggle to believe there is good in them, that they bear the image of the Divine?

And I can't help but wonder why we do this to each other.

If people believe the lie that their lives don't matter, it damages the soul and sometimes kills the body. People don't want to live in a world (read: a family or a church) where they aren't known, accepted, and loved. All people deserve love and justice. Perpetuating hate and fear through destructive theology or political ideology is damaging the collective soul of this worldwide community of humans.

No matter how we were raised or if we cling to faith of any sort, genuine love doesn't have prerequisites. Grace doesn't have qualifying criteria. Compassion has no strings attached. At the end of the day, it is more important to love my neighbors than to expect them to pass a litmus test on morality or religious fervor.

In the past, I've been a coward. I was more concerned with my own acceptance and belonging than standing up to help others receive them. I was wrong to hold back, and I am sorry. These days, I am learning to do better. I'm saying in no uncertain terms that it is wrong for any group of people to be demonized by any institution. I will not stay quiet any longer.

Please hear me: whoever you are, whatever you've done: *you are not bad.* If you've received that message, know it's a nasty, hideous lie. Your dreams, your experiences—your joys and pains and sorrows and traumas and successes—are as unique as the stars in the sky, as varied as the number of hairs on your head.

When did you last look up at the night sky, taking in the wonder of all those twinkling lights? The vastness of that same beauty is contained in your soul, no matter where you've been or what you've been told. And just in case you've been plagued with a terrible case of forgettery, know that you are a priceless commodity. There's not another person on the planet just like you. Even if you're an identical twin, sharing DNA with someone who looks just like you, there's still not another you. You are unique.

> *Unique [yoo-neek]:*
> *adjective*
>
> 1. *existing as the only one or as the sole example; single;*
>   *solitary in type or characteristics*
> 2. *having no like or equal; unparalleled; incomparable*[16]

Gay or straight or something else entirely.
Black, white, or brown.
Freckle-faced or not.
Fat or skinny, tall or short.
Young or old, party animal or happily introverted.

Republican, Democrat, or Independent.

Single, divorced, widowed, or married.

Christian, Atheist, Agnostic, or none-of-the-above.

You have no equal. You are unparalleled, incomparable, a one-of-a-kind gift to this world. There's space at the table for each of us. God and healthy communities have great big hearts and wide open arms. There's plenty of room for everyone to fit. So stretch out, embrace your story, and in doing so, make this humongous mass of humanity just a little more beautiful.

Anyone that makes you feel devalued or ashamed because of your lived experience is not coming from a place of love. When you finally recognize that you are of intrinsic value just because you are a human being, you won't allow anyone to diminish your worth any longer.

In the Christian circles where I used to spend time, people were conditioned by years of toxic theology to believe that they are evil. At the core of their being, people think they were born broken, even to the point of living under a curse. People have learned horrible things like, "God loves me, but must not like me." A lifetime of toxic beliefs and self-destructive habits have convinced us that all we can do is "the best we can" while trying not to screw things up too much.

God in the Gay Bar

There's a beautiful old building I used to drive past that would always catch my eye. The charcoal exterior of the A-frame stands out against the urban backdrop. I've heard the building is just two shotgun-style houses put together, but the design reminds me of the little Methodist church in the town where I was born. One Saturday night, I was invited into its sanctuary to celebrate a friend's birthday.

Creaking stairs greeted me as I turned the decorative metal knob. Music boomed from within. I found smiles all around, people hugging and talking. Some were drinking, most were dancing, and everyone was having a blast. I'd been invited to step into my friend's world. I'd just entered a gay bar for the first time.

It was dark inside, but there was joy in the air. I couldn't shake the sense that this place was a real church. There were bar stools instead of pews, and bartenders standing in for ushers, but I recognized the feeling permeating the club. It was a feeling of safety, of love, of community, of belonging. I walked into that old churchy building, converted into a gay club, and I found God.

The place was a safe haven for those who had been cast aside from most traditional worship. Many had even lost their families. But there, nobody had to fight to be seen or struggle to be afforded the dignity many of us assume is ours from birth. In this sanctuary, my friends were able to be entirely themselves, congregating in the name that is above every name: the name of Love. And that name is too great to ever be labeled "worldly" or "godly," "sacred" or "secular."

Love is just Love.

As the night progressed, the music grew louder and the drinks stronger. The dance floor was filled with familiar faces, and my dearest friends spun, shook, and smiled, weaving themselves in a beautiful tapestry of peace and freedom. It was more than just a party; it was a spiritual experience. My friends were living into their identity, knowing that in a few hours, they would return to straight America. Many would once again hold their authentic selves at a comfortable distance, not wanting to offend their neighbors, co-workers, or those who sit with them on more familiar pews.

I watched them dance and I could feel Immanuel, *God with us*. My friends were the most alive I'd ever seen them. With lifted hearts and heads, the room was filled with laughter and our entire beings overcome with the joy of the Lord. Outside that bar, my friends are judged, cursed, and worse by so-called Christians who are "preaching the truth in love." But inside, they find a shelter from the storm, a community of peace, safety, and love. There's really only one word to describe what they find in that club: God.

And inside that club, they recognize the truth about who they are: valuable, wonderful, made in the image of the Divine. They are reminded that they are, at the deepest level, *good*. After all, that's what God supposedly said when we were created: *this is very good.*

My favorite thing about Jesus is that he came to offer an invitation. He promised that the underdog would have a front row seat in His radical new kingdom, where the last are first. Jesus and those who followed him were square pegs who refused to fit into a round hole, just like Ben's Legos.

In proclaiming really good news to the poor, offering freedom to those in captivity, new sight to those who had been blind, loosening the chains of bondage for the oppressed, embracing women, Samaritans, gentiles, and lepers, the message of Jesus was a big "hell no" to the way things had always been and the lies we've always believed.

When religious people stop expecting people to fit their mold, agree with their politics, or live up to their social expectations, they extend freedom and joy to all of God's people. And isn't belonging what we all want? Isn't that what Christ offers us?

For a group of people so disenfranchised from the Church, a gay bar is a place where everyone is equal. It's a place where "Love is Love" isn't a cliché slogan on a rainbow bumper sticker. It is believed and lived. Love is universal. And the most rebellious thing a student of Jesus can offer another human being is Love.

If you've felt ostracized due to your race, religion, sexuality, gender, disease, or disability, hear me again: *you are not bad.* You don't have to run anymore. You are safe here.

I told you in the beginning that this isn't a book about religion or theology, but a book about people. Still, I cannot write an honest confession or a self-help book without telling you that if you are a part of any setting (religious or otherwise) that is more obsessed with perfection, cleanliness, and cultural norms than making everyone feel welcome, it is toxic. If real people don't feel safe enough to enter the sanitized sanctuary, place of business, or home, it's missing the point.

All any overwhelmed person wants is rest. Love. Mercy for our travels. Friendship. Compassion. Most of all: acceptance. We aren't necessarily looking for answers. Just a place to take off our shoes, bow our heads, and rest, as we breathe in peace that no one can take away. Countless people are hiding in church pews and at dinner tables with their own families, fearing exactly what happened to my friend Ryan. They're confident that if anyone knew their secret, they would be ousted.

In today's context, I think Matthew 25:35-36 would read something like this:

> *I was LGBTQ+, and you welcomed me to the Table. I was homeless, and you gave me a room. I was Hispanic, and you welcomed me. I had HIV, and you visited me. I was a divorcee, and you didn't exclude me from fellowship. I was a woman, and you told me that my voice mattered. I was black, and you listened to me. I was depressed, and you held me close.*

It's time to loosen the death grip on our precious moral stances and open our hands and hearts to those around us who are longing for love and acceptance. Now, more than ever, we should love the person in front of us. We can no longer depend on the church or the government to do what they should. Grace is beckoning each of us to step out, speak up, and make room for everyone.

I wish we could find grace to be unique, to embrace the story of us all, the great big circle and links that bind us together. *Lord, bind us together.* We need the weirdness, the history, the art, the passion, the music, the queerness, and the glitter. We need the richness, darkness like the soil, the dancing, the rhythm, the soul, and the persistence.

Dr. Howard Thurman said, "Don't ask what the world needs. Ask what makes you come alive, and do it. Because what the world needs is people who have come alive."[17]

We need you. Don't back down in your resistance to the lies. You can love and be loved in return, exactly as you are. We need you at the table and there is plenty of room for you.

Come. Let's share our stories. Let's celebrate the ways we are alike, and glory in our differences. Let's listen to the sounds of friendship, harmony, and grace. Grace has made space at the table for all of us.

CRITICALIZIN'

A man with a hump-backed uncle mustn't make fun of another man's cross-eyed aunt.[18]

—Mark Twain

My great-grandfather was a towering man. He had the deepest voice I've ever heard and the biggest heart I've ever seen. He was also educated, speaking at least three languages fluently. Granddaddy's education and mastery of language didn't make him a snob; he was still an unassuming Southern gentleman. But he loved to toy with words, purposely switching letters to create new versions of words or putting the emphasis on the wrong syllable, much to the dismay of his prudish and often-critical wife.

Grandmother grew up dirt poor, and, as a result, seemed to have hardened around the edges. She could find fault in anyone, including her wonderful husband. Grandaddy was the perfect complement for Grandmother. He was soft-spoken, patient, and kind. Opposites, it seemed, did attract.

Grandmother was always on his case. She never seemed to tire of finding some new complaint about Granddaddy. But as the story goes, one day Granddaddy had enough. She followed him up the stairs, like a chihuahua barking and nipping after a tired old hound dog. Apparently, Granddaddy had been criticized for the last time. He turned around at the top of the stairs and, in the most stern voice he probably ever used, said, "Woman, why don't you stop all that criticalizin'?!"

The Voice of the Inner Critic

I left a full-ride scholarship my sophomore year of college to pursue ministry in the church. Of course, people said, "You'll look back in ten years and realize this was the biggest mistake you've ever made." (If only that was the worst of my worries.) Those words rippled into my life for the next fifteen years. Although I'd followed my heart, I hated to disappoint people. The approval fix was a big deal for me.

When things aren't going well, I still hear that voice. When the money runs out before the end of the month, I hear the voice of my inner critic saying, "You should have stayed in school."

It shows up in small, sinister ways. If I ever get sick and have to miss work for more than a day, I feel the pressure of the old-school American male. The pull-yourself-up-by-your-bootstraps, good-old-boy voice says, "Man up! Get your ass to work and stop being a pansy!" I think of the physical toughness and work ethic of my dad and grandfather: they were incredible providers who never seemed to miss work. They even worked holidays and birthdays because a man who never used his sick days was admirable, at least under that old system.

My inner critic shows up any time we need something repaired at home or with one of our cars. My dad can figure out and fix absolutely anything. He's seriously genius-level when it comes to mechanics. When I was a kid, Dad owned a mechanic shop in our tiny town. He repaired and replaced engines, tinkered with lawn mowers, fixed four-wheelers, and more. As a teenager, I watched my Dad teach himself to brick our home. We were building a new home and he didn't want to rely on anyone else.

Me? I struggle to change a tire and can barely construct a Lego house. Sure, I have plenty of other gifts, talents, and abilities. But in my mind, the inner critic has had a love-affair with shame, creating a bastard child I like to refer to as "Mike." (Sorry to all the Mikes reading this.) Mike just seems like the perfect name for a brutish bully who loves to push people around and poke holes anywhere he thinks there might be shame or insecurity.

Mike is a jackass. Like a real one, with long ears, who shows up on bad days or in weak moments, not only to eat your grass but to stand in your backyard, loudly braying at all the ways you are screwing up and missing the mark.

"Missing the mark" was a favorite definition of sin in the Evangelical churches where I grew up. It's interesting how "missing the mark" also naturally shows up when we're talking about perfectionism and shame-based hyper-self-awareness. The truth is, there is nothing sinful about missing the mark of a shame-consumed, fear-based culture.

What about you? How do you criticize yourself when things aren't going well? When that internal dialogue starts to happen, how do you respond? Do your shoulders tense? Does your breath shorten? Your pulse start to race? Do you feel yourself shrinking in shame?

The inner critic is the voice inside your head that tells you all sorts of horrible lies. Because the inner critic is fear-based, it also deals in extremes like "always" and "never." It tells you lies like, "Life is hard and always will be." Have you heard that voice lately? The inner critic wants to prevent us from going after honesty, vulnerability, taking healthy risks, and personal growth.

When was the last time your inner critic showed up? What did he or she say? How do you wish you'd responded? If you could muster the courage to talk back, what would you say? How does it make you feel when you think of combatting the lies you tell yourself?

Living in the *-Ish*

I'm not a perfectionist. I prefer excellence much more. At the end of the day or the completion of a project, my approach is this: "Did you do your best?" If I can answer yes, I'm delighted.

I live my life in the *-ish*. We eat healthy-*ish*, home-cooked meals nearly every night. We raise our children to behave but don't expect them to be robots, devoid of personality. Exercise matters to me, but it's not my number-one priority. And when it comes to my faith, some might call me Christian-*ish* (they'd probably be right). That's okay with me. I live my life 100% in the *-ish* zone because, in a different season of my life, striving for perfection nearly killed me.

I was always hustling to live up to unrealistic expectations and goals that were more than lofty. They were so far from reality, you might call them extraterrestrial (#dadjoke). I would have never put the same pressure on others that I placed on myself. Thankfully, deconstructing my life, spending hours on the couch at my therapist's office, and becoming a parent has started to change everything for me.

I'm not concerned with my kids being perfect. I don't stress if their school portraits aren't worth buying. I don't need my son to make the All-Star team. My daughter loves her dance classes, but I have no expectations of her, other than to have fun, build her self-confidence, and do something she loves. And my wife doesn't desire to have every store credit card she can get her hands on to continually purchase the latest fashion. Some things matter more to us than the external trappings of a "perfect" life. Excellence is good enough for us.

We live in a decent little townhouse that was built in the mid-80's, in a neighborhood that no one is dying to live in. My truck was new in 1995, has no radio, the air conditioning only works on high, and the windshield leaks when it pours down rain. But that same truck belonged to my

Granddad and it allows me to drive my son to school each day, having conversations he'll hopefully remember for a long time.

Sure, we could live in debt up to our ears. Maybe you think I really should force my children to work on their homework or extracurricular activities until they are no longer fun. Some guys love to work out each morning at 4am to fight off the dreaded "dad bod." If those things matter to you, more power to ya. But I now know the life I was missing in the midst of all that never-ending striving. None of those things are nearly as attractive to me any longer.

Criticism's Hidden Gift

As much as I hate striving for approval, I've chosen a strange career path. Writers constantly submit some part of our soul to someone else for approval. It's a bizarre feeling. To some extent, it's an occupational hazard, showing up in the form of harsh comments and emails or social media trolls. But it isn't just writers who experience this. We've all been criticized by difficult people at some point.

Most of us have had a bad boss who never complimented our hard work. Most ministers I know have experienced critical congregations. As parents, most of us have felt the glare of a stranger in the grocery store. We've all shared some part of our personal lives with people, only to have it picked apart by less-than-gracious folks. And for me, it is part of the daily grind. This is my world.

A few years ago, I submitted a piece of writing to a major publication for the first time. It took a lot of guts. When the editor's response arrived via email, I was feeling especially vulnerable and nervous. Instead of turning me down, she offered a great deal of constructive criticism and sent me back to the drawing board, ending with an invitation to send it back over when I was finished. Most new writers would be thrilled, but my thoughts were jumbled and my emotions started to simmer. In the editor's bid to offer constructive criticism, she was direct, to the point of being curt. I began to sway to the all-too-familiar song of shame.

I shut down. I allowed her directness to hurt my feelings, but was embarrassed to admit it. After a long talk with a close friend, I could say it out loud: "I've allowed criticism to feel personal." Have you ever been there? Have you ever allowed someone's negative opinion to define your self-worth? My friend laughed because she knows the business. The piece began to come together as we talked. Even though my writing seemed to be taking off, shame's song of "not good enough" still rang in my ears.

The more I share my story outside my inner circle, the more I open myself to criticizin'. Constructive criticism pushes me to become courageous, to say what I really mean. When I stopped letting that editor's feedback feel so personal, I was able to apply it in a way that made my writing bolder and braver.

Courage is criticism's hidden gift. But just because something is beneficial doesn't mean it is always comfortable. I usually walk into the room ready to do the hard thing. But then my inner critic pipes up, calls me a loser, and ruins my day. Have you ever allowed "this project is missing something" to translate into "you are not enough"? It's my biggest struggle.

I remember working so hard as a kid, bringing home grades most of my friends envied. But in my house, any grade lower than an 85 meant I would be grounded. Average was not good enough. *And neither was I,* I heard. I still hear that voice, over a decade later. *Average doesn't cut it.* If it isn't perfect on the first try, the voice in my head tells me I've failed.

My parents only intended to draw out my full potential, but because of shame and unhealthy striving, my own perfectionism continually chipped away at my sense of self-worth.

In her book, *Banish Your Inner Critic*, Denise Jacobs says:

> *Born from experiences internalized early in life, the Inner Critic is an amalgamation of every critical thing we've ever heard (or thought we heard) from people of influence. In their attempts to push us to conform to the norms of society, parents, older family members or caretakers, teachers, coaches, siblings, peers, and friends are a fount of criticism-filled messages. In our impressionable state, we internalize these criticisms. We model them, viewing ourselves from a place of criticism and judgment. We may even unconsciously emulate the negative beliefs that the people closest to us hold about themselves.* [19]

Sometimes expectations are unrealistic and criticism isn't constructive. It's important to know the difference. Criticism is constructive when it holds a balance of encouragement and challenge. If feedback pushes you to be a better person or improve the quality of your work, that's a good thing. But if criticism makes you feel devalued as a person or smells of shame or fear, it can never be helpful. It is madness to think you can be built up while also being torn down. Shame and fear cannot coexist with love and encouragement.

Life comes with lots of editors: some we invite into our work, and some invite themselves. There are people who peek over our shoulders to tell us exactly what we should have done, when all we were hoping for was compassion. It's tough being criticized at every turn.

As soon as I penned that last sentence, Mike the Inner Critic showed up, whispering his incessant bullshit. "Weak! Pansy! Flower! Snowflake! Sissy!" But are those names true? No. In fact, it takes great strength of character and immense patience to view a sometimes-cruel, critical world with compassion. Plus, when criticism rears its ugly head, we need inner peace. And being a carrier of peace in the face of harsh words is not for the faint of heart.

We experience pain we never asked for—people and institutions cause us harm and distress. We'll be disappointed countless times, but peace is this idea that really bad days come, and we press on. Peace is calm inside when we're in the middle of a raging sea. Being a carrier of peace is a decision: *No point in losing my shit today. It won't do me or anyone else any good.* Peace believes that the promise of a better tomorrow outweighs the difficulty of this particular moment.

Criticism can be painful, whether it comes from inside or out. But inner peace refuses to accept the lie that we're through. Peace believes there is more to the story. When others gossip or whisper, peace doesn't ignore the gnarly details, but is confident in our own resourcefulness and ability to grow. To carry peace is to choose kindness over judgment, compassion instead of criticism, and optimism instead of negativity, *within ourselves.*

Maybe it's your boss, your in-laws, or the stranger at the grocery store who shames you for allowing your two-year-old to have a sugar cookie at 10 a.m. (sometimes you just want to grocery shop in peace, right?). Or maybe it's internet trolls who get some cheap thrill out of picking fights in the comment section. Even if you did invite someone else into your life, only you get to decide how to respond. Let compassion determine how much weight you give those opinions.

No matter what criticism says, we need to show up and tell the truth. We can't compare the chaos we feel inside with the calm we perceive on the outside of other people. We're all good at pretending. Comparison is the enemy of self-compassion. In reality, we are the only people keeping track of all of our imperfections. On bad days, our inner Mike (or whatever your critic is named) can say some really nasty things that we would never-in-a-million-years say to anybody else. I understand the struggle, but *screw you, Mike. I'm done.*

I'm done with all the criticalizin'. Done fighting who I am, just so that I don't offend anyone else. *I'm done* trying to live up to unrealistic expectations, whether internal or external. *I'm done* feeling ashamed for the way I am wired. *I'm done* saying that I love my neighbor while I secretly hate myself. *I'm done* trying to perform just to keep others comfortable.

Truthfully, I've been done for a while, though it's still a battle. I decided to start loving me. I am enough, exactly as I am. I am thankful to be loved by lots of people, but the truth is that I don't need the approval of friends or family in order to love myself.

If you've never fought the inner critic, today is a new day. Say it with me: *today is a new day. I have everything I need for today.* It's time we stop speaking to ourselves from a place of condemnation and self-hatred. The sacred journey from chaos to calm includes living from a place of peace and compassion. It's all inside us already and we don't need anyone's permission to step into it. *So get to steppin'.*

If…

- you're tired of being so hard on yourself…
- you're sick of lies that say you are broken…
- you want to start a journey of embracing this one life you have…

…then join me in fighting the inner critic. It's tough work, but so worth it. After years of practice, most days I can shut Mike's dirty mouth by taking a deep breath and shifting my focus to the inner voice of Love and compassion. You deserve to hear the inner voice of Love, too. It might take time and, if your inner critic is as big of a pain in the ass as mine, it might take support from a good therapist or life coach to kick him to the curb. But no matter what, let shutting him up be a top priority. It's time to *stop all that criticalizin'!*

Seven

THROW EVERYTHING OVER

Don't speak just yet.
Sink into this place.
Sit in your heart.
Close your eyes if you must,
Breathe in,
Breathe out,
Feel the beating of your heart.[20]

—Jennifer Williamson

One Friday night in late May, about twenty-five years ago, my friend's grandpa called. "Hey kiddo, why don't you pack a bag and come spend the night? I've got a surprise for you."

Andy swears he knew what it was right away. He had begged his grandpa to take him fishing for months. All he could think about was how much fun they'd have in the old flat-bottom boat and how many fish they'd catch.

Sure enough, fishing was the plan. Andy could hardly get to sleep and was bouncing like Tigger the next morning. Grandpa placed a finger over his lips, "Shh! Grandma's still sleeping. Don't want to wake the bear!"

When they got to the lake, Andy helped his grandpa load up the boat. By the time they were done, there wasn't much room for them: there were two fishing poles, a jug of water, a lunch box, an ice cooler, and a beat-up coloring book and crayons Grandma had packed, just in case little Andy became bored. There was also a coffee can full of dirt and worms, a net to bring in the catch, a battery-powered radio, sunscreen, life jackets, two paddles, a trolling motor, and Grandpa's wide-brim hat. The boat, to say the least, was pretty full.

Andy was wide-eyed with adventure and possibility as Grandpa pushed them away from the dock. It was sure to be a perfect day, judging by the cool of the morning and the fog on the water. Pretty soon, something else had caught his attention.

Grandpa turned off the motor and turned to see what Andy was giggling about. "Look, Grandpa! This water is *cold*," he said, splashing his feet in it. Surprised and bewildered, Grandpa yelled, "Oh, no! Tell me I didn't forget the drain plug!" The water kept climbing and Andy was getting scared. Grandpa dumped the worms out of the coffee can and frantically started scooping water from around their feet.

It was too late. The little trolling motor wouldn't crank. Grandpa swore under his breath, grabbed a paddle, and paddled hard and fast, desperate to get his grandson to safety. But the weight was slowing them down.

"Throw everything over, Andy!" Grandpa stopped paddling long enough to grab the cooler and throw it in the water as Andy chucked everything he could reach. But the water kept rising. It was too late.

"Come on. We've gotta swim!"

It's my buddy's favorite story. Now a father with kids of his own, Andy looks back with a deep belly laugh and a little tear in his eye at the day he and his Grandpa sank the old flat bottom boat. "But we made it back, nothing hurt but Grandpa's pride."

Throw everything over! My friend says he returns to that advice anytime life feels like too much and he thinks he may drown under the weight of stress, family responsibilities, and work demands.

"You can either hold onto the coloring sheets and can of worms," my friend says, "or you can get your ass back to the pier. Life goes on, even if you're a sopping mess."

Andy's grandpa had all the best intentions, but sometimes good intentions aren't enough when your life starts to take on water. Maybe it's substantial debt or the extra job you no longer need. Perhaps it's your lack of saying "no" to your children, fearing you'll harm them if you don't provide for their every whim and desire. Maybe you came off your depression meds sooner than you needed to and shame is whispering, "You're a failure if you have to call the doctor again." Whatever it is, the only way you're going to make it back when your life has taken on too much chaos is to get rid of all the non-essential cargo.

How? It starts by saying "no." Saying "no" doesn't make you a bad person or a mean parent. "No" isn't a four-letter word. It doesn't make you a bad employee or selfish. Byron Katie says sometimes, saying "no" to people or projects is actually saying a great big "yes" to yourself. When is the last time you said "no" to reclaim your sanity and serenity? Boundaries aren't comfortable when you first start setting them. But they're like the drain plug in Grandpa's old boat: if you neglect them, you'll take on more responsibility and pressure than you can possibly keep afloat.

One of my dear friends is going through an unthinkably hard time: she's watching her marriage disintegrate. She's had to make very tough decisions to protect her safety and sanity. I can't imagine making the painful choice to let go of the person she thought she'd spend her life with. I can see how her boat will be lighter as she lets go of something that's dragging her down. Still, in the midst of a shipwreck, no one says "thank you" for the waves.

Sure, people come running to help in the wake of tragedies they can see, but my friend seemed fine on the outside. There had been no external tragedy; no one saw the dysfunction and toxicity of her day-to-day existence. So not many people came running to her shipwreck. Her chaos is all inside, and it's not easy to find someone to hold your hand while you figure out how to fight that kind of inner war. She was truly overwhelmed.

Two of the most accurate definitions for the word "overwhelmed" come from dictionary.com:

1. *to cover or bury beneath a mass of something, as floodwaters, debris, or an avalanche; submerge:*
2. *to load, heap, treat, or address with an overpowering or excessive amount of anything*[21]

Like my friend, many of us feel like we are slipping beneath the weight of it all. We feel the floodwaters creeping chest-high or hear the sounds of an avalanche chasing us down. Our hopes can get buried underneath an ocean of negativity. Our wildest dreams can seem like pure insanity because our daily lives are so far from what we envision. We're putting one foot in front of the other, dragging ourselves forward, but we are overwhelmed and can barely catch our breath.

Breathing is involuntary; it just happens. We don't have to think about it and it doesn't require focus. We just *do* it. Until we're underwater and that life-giving oxygen gets replaced with something that doesn't belong. Our lungs and nostrils fill up and we begin to choke, cough, and clamor, desperate to breathe again.

Help! We might scream (usually on the inside). *I'm drowning! I can't breathe! I'm overwhelmed!*

The bills are too high!
The baby won't stop crying!
Final exams are a week away!
My wife won't shut up!

My husband never listens!
Work is demanding more than I can give!
I just want to quit!

Have you been there?

It's like running in the Alabama summer, humidity teetering around 90-100%. I love to run, but not in that kind of heat and humidity. It's like trying to breathe underwater or inhaling soup. My lungs and heart curse every pounding footfall. And you can bet I'm not carrying anything heavy with me those days: it's just the essentials.

This morning, as I was nearing my third mile, it felt as though my heart might pound out of my chest and I had a choice – quit or slow down. The truth is, both are valid options. Letting go doesn't mean giving up. It's okay to stop completely and take a break. And sometimes the only way to keep going is to slow down.

When you are running full steam ahead, trying your very best, but feel like you can't possibly go any further, listen to yourself. Don't take another step. If life is really hard right now and you feel completely overwhelmed, you have my permission to let go of anything that isn't giving you life. Let go of the heavy things. Set aside the pressures that are weighing you down. Shut out the critics who aren't in your corner. Set boundaries with those who have bullied or taken advantage of you for far too long.

What is weighing you down? Is it the pain of your past? Is it the terrible way people have treated you or the enormous mistakes you've made? Are you freaked out by an unpredictable future? Does job stress have you teetering on the brink of giving up? Have you lost a precious relationship because of pride or secrets?

If you're anything like me, your arms are full of all the heavy things you've been carrying. Your back hurts from the weight of disappointment and anger, pain and offense. There's no room to embrace love, hope, and empathy. Your shoulders are tense and you are exhausted. Until you let go, you can never fully find yourself or step into your highest purpose. When you're peering over the edge of the cliff, you have to disconnect from the lies that have been embedded in your psyche and tune into love, grace, and compassion. You have to put down the heavy things if you want to create space for real rest.

Do you feel restless? Is there tossing and turning in your soul? Does impatience keep you from sitting with the shakiness and the unknowing? I've been there. We're not taught much about patience after kindergarten, it seems. We rush from here to there. As soon as we get tired of waiting—on people, on answers, on certainty—we get up and leave. We leave our marriages. We leave our jobs. We leave churches. We leave friendships. When we don't find satisfaction or answers as quickly as we think we should, our restlessness nearly drives us mad. Rainer Maria Rilke said it beautifully:

> *Be patient toward all that is unsolved in your heart and try to love the questions themselves, like locked rooms and like books that are now written in a very foreign tongue. Do not now seek the answers, which cannot be given you because you would not be able to live them. And the point is, to live everything. Live the questions now. Perhaps you will then gradually, without noticing it, live along some distant day into the answer.* [22]

We all wrestle with impatience. We want the quick fix, the wonder drug, the easy out. But I don't know many things that are worth having that don't require at least a little bit of hard work.

If the pressure of daily life feels like it might cause your soul to rupture, I get it. And I know that outside of everyday spirituality, the only thing that helped me was doing the hard work of recovery: practicing self-care, listening to the doctor, learning to love myself, and creating a dependable support system. Start with those things, and you'll make significant progress toward finding peace with yourself.

That's where it all begins. When you're in crisis mode, don't feel like you have to force yourself to find immediate peace with God or other people. Those things will come later. But you'll never ease your restlessness—or learn to sit with it—until you learn to create peace with yourself. And most often, that requires letting go. If you want to stop feeling like you're drowning, you have to let go.

"My Give a Damn's Busted"

There's this great old song by country artist Jo Dee Messina, "My Give a Damn's Busted."[23] I firmly believe that each human being receives a certain number of breaths at birth. Right along with the allotted amount of inhales, God gives us a bucket of Give a Damns. (This is a whole new kind of bucket list, people.) Some folks have a surplus of Give a Damns and can keep calm in the face of drama queens, mansplaining, and trying situations. Others have an incredibly limited supply of Give a Damns, and once they're gone, *you'd better run.*

As we journey toward wholeness, we're choosing to step away from constant crisis mode. We're learning that not every friggin' hill is one to die on. We're moving toward deeper connection with our true selves. Doing so will give us the courage to be honest with ourselves and those in our inner circles (at the very least). We will naturally begin to re-prioritize where we spend our time, energy, and focus. Each of these things is a priceless commodity; no matter who we are, we all have a limited amount of each. Run out of any one of these, and we'll begin to float away from the shoreline toward the choppy seas of chaos. And who the hell has time to create unnecessary chaos? *Bye, Felicia.*

There are things we should use a Give a Damn for, and things we shouldn't. My children and my wife are worthy of my Give a Damns. My job gets one, but only because it allows me to pay my power bill and the mortgage. I'll spend a Give a Damn on my car because it gets me to my job so I can pay my water bill and buy groceries for my family. See how this works? There are very few things I should spend my Give a Damn on (and most of the time, it's directly related to the people who live under the same roof as me). There's a shit-ton of stuff that doesn't deserve my Give a Damns. If I can't change something, I sure as hell can't afford to waste my Give a Damn.

Dualistic thinking pushes us to see everything in extremes. Fear-based cable news and social media only make this worse. Not everything in life is an emergency. Not every person is your best friend or your worst enemy. Not every issue needs to be debated. Sometimes, it's just not worth worrying about. Remember, it isn't your job to save everyone, change anyone, or keep the world spinning. Once you recognize what a commodity you have in your Give a Damns, you'll do whatever you can to safeguard them.

Do you remember doing word problems in math class when you were in grade school? They probably sounded something like this: If Sally has five dollars and she buys a sucker for one dollar, how many dollars does Sally have left? You have to budget your Give a Damns just like Sally's dollars.

Here's an example: If someone cuts you off in traffic, you have a choice to make. You can either take a deep breath and keep driving, reserving your Give a Damn for something that truly matters, or you can hold onto your anger and frustration all day.

The third option is to act like my grandpa the day a woman cut him off in traffic and flipped him the bird as she drove past. He waited until they were side-by-side at the next stop light, and rolled down his window. With the whole family in the car, my grandfather leaned his entire upper body out the window, in the middle of the day, placed both middle fingers in the air, and yelled, "Why don't you shove both of these up your ass?!" My grandmother looked on in horror from the passenger seat. (Remember, this was before the days of smartphones and social media. These days, you'd probably end up on an episode of *Cops* for that kind of epic road-rage—or at least on Facebook Live.)

If you waste your Give a Damn on the person who cuts you off in traffic, your co-worker's sideways comment about your shirt, your mother-in-law's criticism of your new car, the fact that the mail is late, or that you didn't get invited to the baby shower, you won't have one left to give when your daughter is sobbing after being made fun of in class. And your daughter desperately needs you to show up.

Letting go is one of the most important parts of this sacred journey. It's a daily practice for a guy like me, who only ever seems to move, add more weight, and keep pushing. As an Enneagram 3w2, my natural bent (especially in un-health) is to get caught up in the *doing*. The dark side of my personality continually tells me to carry more, paddle faster, and refuse to throw anything over.

I need Divine Love to constantly show up, just like it did on my New Year's Eve retreat, and remind me that my worth is found in who I am. Nothing more. God met me there in the sandy sanctuary of Orange Beach, whispering through the wind in the palm fronds, "I've got this. Just rest. Watch what I'm doing. Just listen. Just wait. Just breathe. You can let go."

The quickest way to revert from calm back to chaos is to waste your Give a Damns. And the best way to reserve your Give a Damns? Slow down.

SAUCER AND BLOW IT

Take it easy.

—The Eagles[24]

Boss and Nanny (my mom's parents) have always been two of my dearest friends and mentors. My grandparents' home has often served as a place of solitude during the storms of life. They have passed down all sorts of useful, hard-won wisdom, supported every venture I've tried, and been present with me in both good and terrible times. I'll cherish those memories forever.

If I have any talent as a writer, it's because my grandfather's blood courses through my veins. He was a war correspondent during the Vietnam Conflict and retired from *The Birmingham News* as a night editor when I was a senior in high school. And if I have learned anything about slowing down, it's thanks to Nanny. My grandmother is intentional, careful with her words, and only says what she means. Never rushed or haphazard. Cool, calm, and collected.

Coffee is a staple at my grandparents' home, consumed from dawn until dusk. It's an entirely acceptable beverage for a human from the time they can walk. Black coffee, thick as motor oil, has fueled conversation in our family for as long as I can remember. One of the most significant lessons I learned came from Nanny, who taught me to "saucer and blow it." I'm not sure if this happens anywhere else, but at my grandparents' house, if the coffee is too hot and you just can't wait to drink it, there's a simple fix. You pour it out of the mug and into the saucer, blow on it for a few seconds, wait for it to cool, and slurp it down. *Saucer and blow it.*

Anytime I'm facing a difficult decision (whether the outcome is promising or terrifying), I still pick up the phone and call Nanny. She has listening down to an art and is always present with me in my struggle. Nine times out of ten, Nanny says the same thing: "Stevie, it sounds like you just need to saucer and blow it."

Whether it was giving up a scholarship to pursue Christian ministry, breaking things off with my first fiancé, leaving Bible college to become a sign language interpreter, starting a photography business, or reeling from my wife's hospitalization with postpartum depression, the best advice I've ever received is to take a deep breath and slow down long enough for things to cool down. "Saucer and blow it," in essence, means, don't rush through it.

When you feel out of control, violated, afraid, guilty, alone, embarrassed, ashamed, neglected, or just plain stuck, give things time to cool down. Step back and take a deep breath. Sometimes, there is nothing else to say; things just have to work themselves out. At times, the only thing you can do is saucer and blow it.

As I write this, Boss is dying.

My hero is crumbling into little more than a pile of flesh in a hospital bed. This giant of mine, who has shaped me more as a writer and a man than anyone else, is nearing the end of his natural life. My grandpa, once a powerful physical force, can no longer empty his bladder or recognize his beloved grandson. This brute of a man, who laid the rock foundation of his home without assistance, cannot even lift a spoon to his mouth. The Vietnam War correspondent and well-respected newspaper editor no longer forms coherent sentences. His mind has failed him; his body follows closely behind.

Time becomes so precious when you realize how little you have left with someone you love. Nothing else seems to matter: important podcast interviews, keeping a perfect attendance record at work, taking time to cook real food instead of grabbing something quick. I don't want to miss the chance to hold his hand or wipe his brow. I'm painfully aware of how much time has ticked by while I've been caught up in all the things I'm "supposed to be doing."

At the same time, this deep sadness has made it clear just how harshly I judge my own emotions. Usually, if I feel anything other than happiness, I think something is wrong with me. I have such high and unrealistic expectations that I should always be smiling. But these days, I find myself straddling the guilt-ridden line of wanting him to be free of pain, while my heart silently begs him to stay with me a little longer.

These days, I cannot force a smile. My life isn't falling apart and I am not losing my mind. I'm just really sad. I am permitting myself to slow down and grieve this tremendous loss. I am leaning into this grief and embracing my humanity as I feel my grandfather slipping through my grip.

When my six-year-old son's best friend changed schools, I told Ben, "It's okay to be sad." The kid's parents bought a beautiful new home across town, so my son has lost his favorite friend, the kid who sat next to him every day at lunch. To my little boy, it seems unfair. And although losing a friend he's only known six months pales in comparison to losing the patriarch of our family, the same truth applies to both: *it's okay to be really sad.*

When we prevent ourselves from experiencing the full spectrum of human emotion, it's like we're sawing off an arm or leg with a dull butter knife. It's hard, painful, and unnecessary work. In denying ourselves the right to feel angry, sad, or disappointed—anything but joyful—we're amputating pieces of our souls. This just causes more trauma that will eventually, stubbornly, rise to the surface.

We treat much of our trauma and pain the same way sickness is treated in the Western world. Too often, we treat the obvious symptoms while ignoring the root cause. Over-the-counter cold medicines are designed to treat the effects of the illness: a runny nose, itchy and watery eyes, and congestion. They make us feel better because we can't see the symptoms anymore, but the virus is still wreaking havoc on our systems.

It's the same when we feel overwhelmed. We might use words like anxiety, stress, despair, worn out, exhausted, or just plain done. If we aren't dealing with a genuine psychiatric diagnosis, we're describing intense emotions that we are used to stuffing down or covering up. But what would happen if we stopped trying to squelch or rush through it? What if we asked our emotions what they're trying to communicate to us?

Mark Alan Schelske, in his book, *The Wisdom of the Heart*, offers a very balanced and gracious look at the source of our emotions:

> *If emotions were created as a part of our nature, they're purposeful. This is true regardless of our beliefs about the origin of humanity. If humanity evolved, then emotions emerged through natural selection because they're crucial for survival. If we were created, then emotions are an integral part of the design our Creator gave us. Either way, emotions are vital for a life well lived.*

Schelske goes on to say:

> *At the simplest level, we have emotional responses to our immediate circumstances and internal states. Is this change in circumstance or internal state good or bad for us? If it's good and supportive, healthy emotions should draw us toward the new stimulus with affection, happiness, satisfaction, or*

*joy. If the change is dangerous or threatening, our emotions
are meant to repel us from the stimulus with responses like
anxiety, fear, disgust, and hate.*[25]

I wonder how we might better manage our response to people and situations if we viewed our emotions as messengers rather than allowing them to control us. We say things like, "I *feel* stressed." Or, "I *feel* overwhelmed." But what's beneath the feeling? What's causing the inner turmoil? Is it fear of the future? Is there an actual untreated psychiatric diagnosis? Is it anger? Disappointment? Is it lack of sleep? Is low blood sugar? (Come on, don't tell me I'm the only one who loses it when I get *hangry*!)

What would happen if we permitted ourselves to be human? Notice that I didn't say "permitted ourselves to expect the whole world to stop while we grieve." And it's not okay to drown yourself in numbing behaviors and addictions. Neither of those are healthy options. But we certainly have the right to sit in the midst of suffering and work through the feelings in healthy ways.

We don't have to toughen up. We don't have to pretend we aren't crying. We don't have to "be a man." Your emotions belong to you—our emotions belong to each of us. The trick to this, and to all of life, is learning how to show up where we *need* to when we don't *feel* up. To do the tasks we have to do, based on the roles and responsibilities we have, without ignoring our emotional needs in the process.

It's all a balancing act. Lose control and allow your emotions to run rampant? You risk losing your job or the respect of those who depend on you. Stuff your feelings, pretend nothing is wrong, and push through the pain, full steam ahead? Eventually, you'll implode, potentially causing even more harm to yourself and others. The key is being kind to yourself, honest with the people in your inner circle who need to know what's going on, and working through whatever trials you face with self-compassion.

In grief, each day is different. To embrace the tension of my grandpa's last days on earth, I had to get quiet, put down the phone, and intentionally walk away from empty busyness that kept me from being present with my family. Now, I practice mindfulness by asking myself what I need today. If I have a big meeting at work that I cannot miss without putting my job in jeopardy, I may choose not to visit my grandfather before work. I know that doing so would zap all of my energy, productivity, and attention. The wise choice would be to visit him after the meeting instead. On the flip side, if my grandfather has taken a turn for the worst, I have to remind myself that I always have choices. There may be consequences if I miss the staff meeting, but only I can decide which is the right choice for me at any given moment. Grief, like life, is complicated. I can't stop my granddad from dying, but I can keep it from destroying me.

When we feel about as strong as an eggshell, the first courageous thing we can do is to ask for help. Finding a safe person means reaching down deep into our souls and mustering the courage to connect with someone we trust. Someone who makes us feel valued, seen, and heard. Whether it's a family member, a friend, or an unbiased professional, we need someone to help us navigate life.

Effective or Efficient?

In my work with people moving from chaos to calm, I have noticed a big misunderstanding between the words "effective" and "efficient." "Effective" *feels* much better than "efficient," right? Efficient feels impersonal—robotic even. But I think most of us say *effective* when we mean *efficient.* Why? Because we've bought into the lie that says to make the most substantial impact we must do more than anyone else, even though we all have the same number of hours in a day.

Beat the competition.
Buy the bigger house.

Lease the sports car.
Land the new promotion.
Slay the dragon.

But do you know the secret to living your most efficient life? *Slow down.*

I know, it makes no sense, right? You want me to teach you to how to increase your focus. You want one quick tip to better productivity.

Here it is—*slow down.*

An agriculture magazine shared this story:

> *A woodsman was once asked, "What would you do if you had just five minutes to chop down a tree?" He answered, "I would spend the first two and a half minutes sharpening my axe."* [26]

If we never slow down enough to "sharpen the axe," the blade loses its edge. It takes more and more energy to do the same amount of work because the axe isn't in top condition. It's worn out, dull, and eventually becomes useless. That's why it's more efficient—and more effective—to slow down, rest, and sharpen the axe.

There are plenty of books on all the ways to speed up and do more. If that's what you're looking for, go read those. This is a book about how to be the healthiest human you can. And in order to do that, you've got to stop expecting yourself to be a machine.

Slow down. I don't mean stop. I don't mean you have to sit and watch everyone pass you by, but I do know that, as a human, you can't keep pushing forever. You can't keep going without refilling and expect not to face burnout.

If you're overwhelmed today, hear me: *it's okay to slow down*. When you are drowning, the best advice I can give you is to cast off the things that feel too heavy. Let go of the unrealistic expectations. Stop running and give yourself time to breathe.

It doesn't matter who you are. A mother of three who is desperate to lose weight? A pastor whose congregation has shrunk from 300 to 30? An entrepreneur bogged down by the business side of things when all you want is to serve people? A college student crushed by the weight of anxiety and a heavy class load? Whatever the case, please don't wait until you're entirely overwhelmed before you do something about it.

My advice? *Slow down.*

"But, how?!"

Get a piece of paper and a pen. Ready?

Make three columns:

1. What I have to do.
2. What I feel pressured to do, but don't want to do.
3. What I want to do.

Now, before we look at what goes in these columns, take a deep breath. Are you ready to get gut-level honest about all the things that keep you moving too fast?

No? Then come back later. *Don't waste your ink.*

Yes? Then, after you read the instructions for each column, start writing. *Tell me everything.*

Once you've put it all down on paper, take another deep breath, hold it for a few seconds, and slowly release.

What I have to do

This column is for things you cannot function without. If you don't work, you cannot pay your power bill, you cannot cook supper, and you cannot feed your children. So you *have to* work.

But do you have to work 80 hours per week? Can you pay the bills by only working 40–50? Get honest. What do you *really* have to do?

Examples:

1. Take care of my family.
2. Eat.
3. Sleep.
4. Pay the bills.

What I feel pressured to do, but don't want to do

This column is likely overflowing with things you don't actually *want* to do, but feel stuck with. If you're like most people (including me), you may have run out of space for everything you would love to get off your plate.

This is where you have to get nekkid. This list can be challenging to let go of because these things often come from our own internal struggle with fear, shame, and guilt. Some of the things in column two are perfectly harmless, but are they adding to your sense of calm or of chaos? Only you can answer this question. There's nothing wrong with having a clean house, a social life, and a strong sense of religious tradition. Unless those pressures aren't healthy for you. It's all about your motivation.

Examples:

1. Going out with coworkers for drinks every Thursday.
2. Teaching Sunday School again this year.

3.   Homeschooling the kids.

4.   Coaching your kid's Little League team.

5.   Having a perfectly clean house.

6.   Holding onto the religious traditions of my family/childhood.

What I want to do

This is one sad column. For a lot of us, this is where dreams go to die (cue the sad trombone). Most of us put off what we really want while we fill our schedules with what we feel pressured to do. Sure, we'll do it *someday*: after we graduate, get married, get promoted, have kids, after the kids start school, after the kids finish school, after retirement. Before long, we've missed decades and all we have left to look forward to is crossword puzzles, daytime television, and AARP discounts.

Even though we sincerely want to do these things, we put them off, telling ourselves to wait for more money or time. But time is a commodity we are constantly losing. We'll never have more than we do right now. *How's that for encouragement?*

And when it comes to money, maybe we just need to get creative. If we're honest, there are probably ways to trim budget so we can do what makes us come alive. We can probably work on that passion project *and* make a little side money.

Examples:

1.   Take the family on a dream vacation.

2.   Renew your vows.

3.   Run a marathon.

4.   Adopt a baby.

5.   Finish the degree.

6.   Write the book.

7. Visit Europe.
8. Form a non-profit.
9. Record an album.
10. Start a podcast.

Where do I even begin?

Okay, you've got three lists now. Did ya shuck down and get nekkid? Were you gut-level honest with yourself? Good job. Take a deep breath.

No, really; take a deep breath. This is hard work.

You might feel better already, seeing what your real priorities are and what you really don't want to do. Or you might feel *more* overwhelmed and wonder where to even start with all of this. How do you take this information and use it to slow down?

The answer is different for everyone. I think the simplest place to start is by answering this question: *what can you take off your plate **today** to give yourself more space to breathe and just be?*

It's probably going to be something from your second column. Start by taking off some of the internal pressure. Now that you recognize things in this column aren't essential, what are you willing to cross off? You might feel a little guilty at first or even disappoint someone, but it will move you toward calm and away from chaos.

Once you've eliminated a few things, look at the three lists we just created, and think about how to prioritize your responsibilities and passions. Find a balance to both working and living.

Remember when I said you can find creative ways to live your passion and make a little money on the side? That's exactly what this book is for me. I'm no full-time writer. Sure, I'd love to be, but right now, I spend thirty hours a week as a sign language interpreter because it pays my bills and gives me a little free time to do what I love. Time and money are most people's excuse for slowly falling asleep while they are wide-ass awake; don't do it.

Getting nekkid about your needs and wants is a powerful way to prioritize your life. Not only will you be able to slow down and live your truth, but you'll also begin to enjoy yourself. And, since you'll leave plenty of time open to sharpen your axe, you'll find increased efficiency in the things that matter most, plus more creativity, confidence, and calm in every area of your life.

Finally, now that you've examined and re-established priorities, think about your responsibilities. When it comes to all the things you truly *have* to do, set some boundaries and don't budge. There will always be more work to do—more paperwork, more phone calls, more email. But you don't have to keep the same pace anymore. You can pursue those dreams and enjoy your life. Because the only way to create the life you've always wanted is to slow down.

nine

QUIET AF

If we were not so single-minded
about keeping our lives moving,
and for once could do nothing,
perhaps a huge silence
might interrupt this sadness
of never understanding ourselves
and of threatening ourselves with death.
Perhaps the earth can teach us
as when everything seems dead
and later proves to be alive.[27]

—Pablo Neruda

On the final day of our beach getaway, my wife offered to whisk the children off on an adventure, giving me four uninterrupted hours to write. When someone offers the gift of quiet, you take it. For most of us, it doesn't come often enough. (You may have to ask for that time, too. It's your right and responsibility to speak up and say what you need.)

Sure, I could have binge-watched my latest TV addiction or drowned in the neverending sea of social media, but none of that is stillness. And I know that soon enough, these children, whom I adore, will return with their needs and laughter and "help me!" and giggles and "Daddy, could you...?" and running through the middle of the living room. So I settled in.

There's a little pine thicket near the back porch that can't be very old; the young trees rocked to the rhythm of the rain that tap danced down the stairs like Gene Kelly. Fifty yards away, the sea oats swayed in the breeze, bidding me to come and follow suit, as the wind sang its siren song and my coffee (or was it whiskey?) warmed my bones.

Two-hundred-forty minutes ticked by in less than a blink. My kids were back in all their noisy, messy glory. But that much-needed stillness was so good for my soul.

It's good for yours, too. So make it a priority to cultivate quiet every chance you get. Whether that means paying for a babysitter or creating a "kid swap" with neighbors and friends, figure out a way to make it work. If you're in a relationship, rotate who keeps the kids and give your partner a couple of hours of quiet. Whatever you do to cultivate calm, always say "thank you" for the gift of stillness. And be intentional with every calm moment you're given. It is priceless.

Most of us don't slow down long enough to catch our breath. We're always running because we've bought into the lie that our worth is determined by what we do and how much we produce. But the truth is that our worth is found in who we are. We run here and there, so focused on our checklists that we forget the most basic of human functions: *breathing*! Taking time to just breathe looks different for everyone, but could include meditation, contemplation, prayer, yoga, fishing, or a simple walk around the block.

One of the biggest mistakes people make on the journey from chaos to calm is trying to do everything at once. They want to change their diet, exercise, meditate, get a life coach, and start journaling on day one. And the best advice I can give you is to take a deep breath, take it one step at a time, and, like we talked about in the last chapter, *slow down*. Don't try to get from point A to point Z today. Just take a deep breath and the first step.

Creating space

When I was growing up, my dad always had a massive garden. Even though we lived in a typical suburban neighborhood, each summer, the garden took up half the backyard. But you never heard us complain—fried okra, fresh from the garden? *Are you kidding me? Heaven on a plate!* Mama would dump them out of the deep fryer onto paper towels to sop up the grease while my brothers and I fought over who would sample that garden goodness first. Then there were green beans, yellow squash, tomatoes, and even a watermelon or two.

But before we could enjoy those wonderful fresh vegetables, Dad had to clear a plot. And before the beans or the squash ever poked their little green heads up out of the ground, Dad would be down on his hands and knees, pulling weeds. Stubborn and fast-growing, they spread like wildfire. "You have to stay on top of the weeds," he'd say, "or they will choke out the good stuff before it ever takes root.

Creating something life-giving is not for the faint at heart. My dad has always been the hardest-working man I know, so it makes sense that he'd find pleasure in doing something as difficult and time-consuming as growing and maintaining a garden. For most of us, creating space in our lives feels like a lot of work. Cultivating a life of stillness begins by clearing a plot, too.

A Fig Tree...Without Figs?

There's a story in the Bible about a tenant farmer with a fig tree that produced no figs (Luke 13:5-9, MSG). Lame, right? What good is a fruit tree without any fruit? After three years of producing no figs, the landowner was ready to cut it down. But the farmer begged the landowner to give him one more year to see if he could get it to produce fruit. The landowner gave in, so the farmer cleared around the roots of the tree and spread manure all around.

This story is messy and beautiful for two reasons:

1.   The gardener has compassion on the fruitless tree and asks for more time to cultivate it. He knew it could live up to its purpose, given a little more time and care.
2.   Poop produces. Sure, it stinks and makes a big mess—it's nothing more than the waste of an animal—but sometimes the biggest mess yields the greatest growth.

I've never grown a garden of my own, but every six months or so, my wife and I spend a weekend morning purging excess stuff from our home. Decluttering is time-consuming and just plain annoying. And much like weeding my dad's garden, it's one of those tasks you have to stay on top of, otherwise the place gets overgrown with things that don't matter. One of the perks of living in a two-bedroom townhouse is that the stuff never really has a chance to pile up for too long. Because we occupy such a tiny living space, we simply cannot store anything we don't need.

No matter what my role—life coach, pastor, author, or teacher—I love helping people create more space in their lives. Whether we know it or not, most of us want more room for things that nourish us. People will usually say something like, "I'd like more time," but what they mean is, "I'd like more time with the good stuff of life." We want time and space to do the things we're passionate about with the people we love. So how do we guarantee this will happen in our lives? It all starts with clearing a plot.

Shh...

Two years after I almost died, a car wreck threatened to destroy our marriage. It was September of 2014. My little boy, Ben, was turning three, and Sweet Caroline was about five months old. I had been in recovery, rebuilding my life, for two years. But, sadly, I slipped back into my old routine of pushing, performing, and moving to the point of extreme exhaustion. I was working two jobs and pulling 60-hour weeks with two little ones and my sweet wife at home.

For some reason, I had borrowed Lindsey's car that Saturday morning. I was so tired from working till midnight the night before and having to be back by 6:00 AM., the kind of tired that gives coffee the stank eye and laughs in the face of a nap. I only fell asleep for a second, but it was a second too long. The impact of the other car jolted me awake.

I couldn't believe this was happening. We were covered in debt, and I'd picked up an extra twelve-hour shift that morning to try and make ends meet. The worst part? The insurance agent promptly reported, "Mr. Austin, your auto insurance lapsed three weeks ago." In my busyness, I had completely forgotten to renew it.

I called to deliver the bad news to my wife. I felt like all I ever gave her was bad news and a lack of presence. But this was too much. I can still hear her say those heavy words: "I'm taking the kids to Florida for a while until we can figure things out."

I hadn't cried in front of my dad in years, but that day, standing in my parents' driveway, telling him my marriage might be over, I sobbed. I realized that, in my constant struggle to be good enough, I had neglected the most precious person in my life.

While my wife was packing her bags for Florida, I started wracking my brain for something I could do to find some semblance of peace for us.

I knew I had to do something different. The same old thing just wasn't working anymore. Desperate times call for desperate measures, right?

For me, desperate meant getting really quiet. I spent that Labor Day weekend in silence in a monastery in Cullman, Alabama. I mean, it was *quiet AF*. I disconnected from everyone and everything I'd been using as a distraction from what was going on inside of me, just like I'd done in the psych ward. But where the psych ward deals with the brain, this trip was for my soul and body.

In my borrowed cell, my soul found stillness and my body was able to rest. I turned off my phone. I only brought a couple of books, pens, and a journal. If I was ever going to redeem my marriage, I first had to rediscover myself. It was time to get nekkid again.

This is why Brennan Manning's words are so powerful: "Silent solitude makes true speech possible and personal. If I am not in touch with my own belovedness, then I cannot touch the sacredness of others. If I am estranged from myself, I am likewise a stranger to others."[28]

I learned that when I'm not in touch with my belovedness, I'm more susceptible to the lie that my worth is found in what I do, create, and give. As much as I wanted to believe I had recovered and was in a great place, I wasn't in a healthy frame of mind at all. I had worked to have my ego stroked by how well I performed and how loudly the crowd applauded. A weekend of stillness allowed me to realize that and take a step toward healing my marriage. That weekend of silent contemplation reminded me again that I am loved *because* of who I am, not *in spite* of it.

In *8 Habits of Love*, my friend Ed Bacon talks about the habit of stillness:

> *Life comprises both ordinary and extraordinary moments.*
> *When we need to imagine, dream, plan, strategize and*
> *nurture ourselves and others, this is hard to achieve when*

we react to everyday life with anxiety. When we are full of fear, being open-hearted becomes virtually impossible. We are stalled. We cannot grow or find imaginative solutions. Yet, this habitual fear is not always easy for us to recognize. It takes on many masks.[29]

Maybe you have three children under the age of five. Perhaps you are convinced your spouse has been wrongly imprisoned. Maybe you're walking through bankruptcy, divorce, or grieving as you witness a loved one deteriorate before your eyes. Whatever your version of chaos, creating moments of stillness can help you cultivate calm.

Ed Bacon goes on to say:

Over the years, I've come to view reaching daily stillness the way I view my morning shower and toothbrushing. I spend an hour each morning in stillness, which for me, is my deepest form of praying, and I don't want to enter my day without this act of spiritual, mental, and emotional hygiene.

Rev. Bacon is right. Just like a refreshing shower or a cleansing tooth-brushing, my soul craves the washing of its inner-sanctum by stillness. Even if you don't find yourself swept away by the undertow of tragedy, the very chaos of daily life begs for a regular dose of stillness.

For me, stillness means a trip to the local Catholic church each year on the morning of September 21st, the day I nearly died by suicide. I know very little of the Catholic tradition, but the prayer garden on the church grounds beckons me. As I observe the statue of Mary, the flowers, and the candles, I remember the Biblical story of Jesus in the Garden of Gethsemane. His soul was in chaos and he had to find stillness before the unthinkable next steps we read about in the Gospels.

As I'm invited into stillness in my own prayer garden, I also remember the day that defined chaos for me. You cannot fully appreciate calm without living through the chaos; the two are intrinsically woven together. It's why I believe the human journey really is all about death and resurrection. Chaos and calm. It's all an ebb and flow. And Hope is the anchor that reminds us calm is waiting on the other side of chaos.

Like Ed, I practice a daily habit of calm. Each morning, I put in my earbuds and turn on my favorite guided meditation app (there are quite a few to choose from). I don't get stuck on how long I should or shouldn't meditate—to me it's about the intention. Sometimes, it's just a few minutes. Other times, it's half an hour or more. However long I spend there, I count it a success. I give myself permission to be human in all things.

If the idea of meditation trips you up, let's make it simple. If you're exhausted, stressed, or scattered, the best meditation in the whole world is a damn nap. Close your eyes and shut out all the distractions. Step away from the digital noise of television and social media and get quiet for a while. It is amazing to me just how much a nap can help. When I'm feeling stressed, impatient, or just plain cranky, an hour of shut-eye is often exactly the reset my body needs.

On, Not Up

Somehow, we get in our heads that we need to have it together all the time. Is it just me? I tell myself that I must be "up" all the time, but that's a crock. Anyone who has lived through a difficult time knows that "just choosing joy" doesn't always do it.

One piece of tough love my friend Sue has given me a few times during the years is this: when it comes to leadership and life, she says, "You don't always have to be *up*, but you always have to be *on*." Even when that advice isn't comforting, it's true. Whether I'm working as a sign language interpreter, life coach, or speaker, most people don't care what kind of bad day I've had, about my lack of sleep, or even that my dog was just run over (*insensitive jerks*). They aren't concerned with whether I am feeling "up," as long as I am "on" and capable of doing my job.

In case you haven't gotten the memo yet, you're human. As such, your energy and mood will vary from time to time. It's crucial to give yourself permission to be down sometimes. At the same time, listening to your mood and energy signals will help you know when you need an extra dose of stillness. Sometimes, in order to be "on" when you're having a tough day or week, you need to prioritize *more* time to refresh. Remember the woodcutter? When you feel extra grumpy, extra stressed, or extra down, take a look at your schedule, pencil in some quiet time, and go sharpen your axe.

I love the way stillness takes all the social norms and cultural expectations and turns them upside down. It doesn't make sense in our got-it-together, keep-it-together world of constantly going, pushing, moving forward, always up, always on. But it *does* make sense for our bodies, souls, and minds. If we want to be healthy and able to do what really matters, we have to stop and give ourselves permission to listen to our own breath.

How to Not Get Hit by a Train

When I was a kid, we learned lots of lessons in threes. For example, if there's a fire, what do you do? *Stop, drop, and roll.* Good job. Most sermons in the little Southern Baptist church of my childhood also had three points. I guess it's easier to remember three than, say, Martin Luther's *95 Theses.*

One of the most memorable three-point lessons from childhood is what to do when you approach a railroad crossing. Do you remember the rule? *Stop, look, and listen.* If you don't want to get hit by a train, these three habits are vital. The results of *not* following these instructions can be cat-astrophic. Trains come at us with enormous momentum and if we aren't paying attention, terrible things can happen.

During my formative years, I recognized just how powerful trains are. When I was a young boy, Papaw Thompson would load me up in his old, white Datsun pickup with the brown vinyl interior and drive us down to the train track beside Yellowleaf Creek. Papaw would pull the truck onto the gravel access road next to the tracks. He would park near the tiny signal house, raise one finger in the air, and with a childlike sparkle in his eyes, whisper, "Now, you wait right here."

No matter how many times I'd seen the trick, I was always amazed at how the train flattened a perfectly good penny. Papaw would place the shiny copper coin on the track while the train was still a good way off, and after the choo-choo rolled over it, the penny would be pressed paper thin.

That penny was nearly crushed beneath the weight of the locomotive; its shape was forever altered by the relentless smashing of the engine, coal cars, and caboose. And if you don't stop, look, and listen, a train will treat you the same way. Trains are no respecter of persons.

When is the last time you stopped, looked, and listened? It can save you from a great deal of trouble. Whether your soul feels clogged, anxiety is squeezing your brain, depression's black dog is hounding you day and night, or you're just not sure you can handle the stress much longer, please stop, look, and listen.

Stop

Stop performing for the approval fix. Stop trying to live up to the un-realistic expectations of others. Stop trying to keep the world spinning.

Remember what Sue says, "The merry-go-round has a motor. All you have to do is get on and ride."

Look

Look around. What do you see? Piles of responsibility and resentment? Loads of busyness? Five-mile-long lines of chores and demanding people? When is the last time you shifted your focus and looked for the beauty in everyday life? When did you last notice the deep blue of your wife's eyes or the way your husband's beard is beginning to grey? When did you stop long enough to appreciate your son's homework or watch your daughter twirl in the backyard like a ballerina? Look around—what are you grateful for?

Listen

Listen to the voice beneath the chatter. Stop talking long enough to appreciate the gift of silence. Feeling stuck? Listen to the answers inside of your soul; they're longing to show you a better way. Ed Bacon refers to stillness as "the level beneath quiet." It's the place down in the deepest sea of your soul, where the waves can no longer distort or distract. Get quiet and listen to the voice of God—the voice of Love and Belonging and Peace—in the midst of a life that seems to never slow down.

Stop striving. Look for goodness. Listen to the truth of your being.

Life is either a gift or a long series of moments where you hold your breath until the next disaster strikes. I'm choosing to slow down, keep my eyes peeled, and my heart open to the blessing of each ordinary day, believing that I was made for more than just the next trainwreck.

Returning to Stillness

From my journal:

> *Here I am, sitting in this brown leather recliner, holding a book. I feel the dryness of the pages against my fingers and notice the refreshing air from the ceiling fan, lightly breathing against my skin. The cotton of my shirt brushes against my arms, and I sense the tightness of my shoes on my feet. I can feel the weight of the book in my lap and my coffee cup warming my left palm. Here I am, breathing calmly. Here I am, resting my shoulders, letting go of the tension in my eyebrows and my jaw. Here I am, relaxing into this moment.*
>
> *When I get quiet enough, I can hear the little bird singing its song outside on the tree branch. I can listen to the hum of the air conditioner, and I'm pretty sure there's a drip in my bathroom faucet. Whoever said "silence is golden" was right.*

When is the last time you got quiet for just five minutes? Maybe the thought of meditation overwhelms you. Perhaps you're like a friend of mine and, because of past trauma, deep breathing techniques freak you out. What if you just sat, closed your eyes, put your feet on the floor, your hands in your lap, and listened? When we become intentionally quiet in the natural world, it allows us to listen to ourselves on a different level. Some might call it a spiritual level. We finally create space to listen to those big questions that are gnawing at our souls. We can hear the dreams, the questions, the fears, the doubts, the desires...but only by getting quiet.

Reticular What?!

"You ever heard of the reticular activator?" I was at Sue's house, checking on her after a recent medical procedure. (Sue and I are sort of like characters from the 90's sitcom, *Home Improvement*. I'm Tim Taylor and she's Wilson, the neighbor on the other side of the fence. Sue is used to my confused looks and mile-long stares as she pontificates about deep and mind-boggling truths of the Universe.

"The reticular what?!" I asked, my voice an octave higher and full of confusion.

The Encyclopedia of Neuroscience defines the reticular activating system this way:

> *Humans have three sleep and arousal states: waking, asleep (resting or slow-wave sleep), and asleep and dreaming (paradoxical, active, or rapid eye movement sleep). These states are controlled by the reticular activating system located in the mesopons, which interacts with descending reticulospinal and ascending hypothalamic, basal forebrain, and thalamocortical systems.*[30]

Can we all breathe a collective *WTF?* Basically, the reticular activator is the part of your brain that notices things.

Sue went on to tell me about buying her red convertible a few years before. She had never noticed so many red convertibles on the road until she owned one herself. Her reticular activator had subconsciously been weeding out unnecessary information, allowing Sue to focus on driving and getting to her destination. But now that she owned a red convertible of her own, suddenly, it seemed there were many more!

I don't notice the hum of my air conditioner the majority of the time. But when it's time to hit "record" on my next podcast episode, you can bet I know exactly how loud the vent is in my office. *Damn reticular activator.*

Stillness sharpens the reticular activator of the soul. As you engage your reticular activator through a regular stillness practice, you hone your ability to notice. And the opposite is true, too: you fine-tune your skills at culling distraction. Coming to stillness, you filter through the white noise of busyness and unnecessary bullshit so you can notice what your soul is trying to tell you. It makes space to allow the truth of your being to grow. It is watering the ground of your soul, allowing goodness and truth and light and calm to grow.

As I sit in silence, more often than not, a smile curls around my lips and I think *this is good.* All of this may sound silly to you. Maybe you read these words and think, *who cares about your recliner and the hum of a ceiling fan?* The ceiling fan is not the point. *Wax on, wax off.* The purpose of this exercise is to realize how many regular moments we miss every day because we are so busy, trying to get to the next appointment, next meeting, or next event.

My challenge for you, right now, if at all possible, is to close this book and sit still for five minutes. Do nothing other than getting quiet and observing. What do you notice? Is it sunshine through the window? Your partner snoring in the next room? The buzz of a fluorescent light fixture above you? Or the rump-a-tum-tum of your heartbeat? Note every single thing you observe for five minutes and when you finish, take a moment to write it all down. Getting quiet in the natural world is a crucial step toward creating calm on the inside.

Ten

A DOG NAMED DUDLEY

When will you have a little pity
for every soft thing
that walks through the world,
yourself included?

—Mary Oliver[31]

I spent the first decade of my life in the country. Boss and Nanny owned a large plot of land in rural Alabama and we only lived a couple of miles away. There were always five or six junk cars lined up by the barn. As a kid, I couldn't figure out why they didn't just sell them or fix them up, but now I understand: Boss and Nanny grew up just after the Great Depression. There was a lot of fear leftover from those lean years. You never knew what you might need, so you couldn't get rid of anything. Even if it was rusty enough to give you tetanus from twenty feet away.

Come to think of it, the whole thing seems a little bizarre now. Boss and Nanny would slice up apples and leave them to dehydrate in the back windows of the cars. Of course, I was a kid, so I didn't really care. After all, my cousin and I spent long afternoons playing in those old beaters, pretending to be racecar drivers. (*Duh!* What else would you play in a rusted-out Toyota Celica?) Plus, we had snacks when we wanted them.

My grandparents had an old mutt named Dudley who was part of the family. One afternoon, Dudley didn't come home, but that was nothing to worry about. He was a country dog and roamed free, sometimes following my cousin and I around the property, sometimes off hunting rabbits or female dogs in heat.

But he didn't come home that night.

Or the next night.

Or the next day.

A couple of days *was* cause to worry, even for a free-range mutt like Dudley. Finally, it hit Boss: "Stevie and Candy were down there in those damn cars..." (*BTW, don't go gettin' too big for your britches and think you can call me Stevie. Boss and Nanny are the only ones to call me that.*) He headed down by the rickety barn and started searching his fleet of rust-buckets. Sure enough, he found Dudley dehydrated and half-dead in the backseat of one of those Celicas.

The poor mutt must have jumped in when we'd left the door open; we never had a clue he was in there. Thankfully, it wasn't the middle of the Alabama summer and the windows were pretty much always cracked. Oh, and there were those dehydrated apples in the back window for him to survive on. That's probably what saved his little cur-dog life. Boss and Nanny nursed poor old Dudley back to health and renamed him Lazarus. But he was never quite right after that. *Okay, they didn't really rename him Lazarus, but wouldn't that be awesome?!*

Most people haven't accidentally left an innocent dog in a broken-down car that smells like apples. But I wonder how many folks act like they've reached junker-status and parked themselves near the barn, door hinges stuck and paint fading fast? See, we require regular maintenance to run efficiently, too. We have to charge the battery, fill the gas tank, and change the oil. Otherwise, our souls become rusted shut, our brains struggle to operate through a fog of exhaustion, our relationships suffer, and our bodies fall into disrepair. Now that we've slowed down and caught our breath, cultivating a lifestyle of self-care is the best way to stay on the path from chaos to calm.

Take Care

I love to write letters. Sure, email is more efficient, but taking the time to craft a handwritten note and send it to someone I care about adds an exceptional touch. Often, when I pen a letter, I end it with two words: *take care.* I also use those words at the end of a conversation with clients or friends, or even someone I've chatted with casually in the hallway at work. For a lot of us, it's just something we say instead of "sincerely" at the end of the letter or "goodbye" at the end of a conversation.

Take care.

Take good care of yourself.

But those words communicate something deeper, something more powerful. After all, we take great care of the things that matter to us. Our children. Our homes. Our relationships. The antique car we inherited (unless you're Boss or Nanny). As kids, we took care of special dolls or baseball card collections. We place *care*-ful attention on the things we value.

But what about our lives?

John Wesley famously asked the question, "How is it with your soul?" We already talked about everyday spirituality, so you know I'm not talking about going to church. But do you read books or listen to lectures/podcasts that feed your soul? Do you take walks in nature to remind yourself that there is more to this life than the nine-to-five hustle and bustle? Do you spend time in silence or in laughter or whatever it is you need? In the day-to-day, how do you take care of your soul?

You Can't Do It All

In one grief-stricken weekend in my hometown, I heard of two deaths by suicide and two others longing to die. Friday morning, news broke of an 8th-grade girl in our town who died by suicide. And within twenty-four hours, I received calls from two friends dealing with suicidal thoughts. Then, I got the terrible call from a friend who lost a brother to suicide. Yes, all in one tragic weekend.

What do we do when our hearts are tearing in multiple directions, and we want to help but are being triggered at the same time? What do *I* do in that situation, where people look to me as an expert on mental health because I share my story, but sometimes hearing about others' struggles is too much for me? What do we do when life feels too heavy?

We have to take care of ourselves first.

I know, it sounds selfish, right? I wanted to help in each situation. I wanted to comfort my friend who had just lost her brother; after all, I know what it's like to lose a beloved family member to suicide. I wanted to reach out and "fix" things for my friends who were struggling hardcore, because I am intimately acquainted with those kinds of thoughts. And I wanted to be a beacon of hope for our community in the wake of this young girl's death.

But I couldn't fix any of this. A few years ago, I would have stretched myself beyond any healthy or wise limits and tried to be in four places at once. And my family and my mental health would have suffered as a result. These days, I'm much more aware of healthy and wise limits. So I did my very best to help where I could. I tried to offer hope and tell the truth, but also set some solid boundaries. It doesn't mean I didn't care—on the contrary, I feel *awful* when I can't fix it for other people. My heart aches and I battle serious guilt. But I've learned I can't let those feelings make my decisions. I'm human, too.

Self-Care Saves Lives

That tragic weekend, even as I helped where I could, I had to be extra-diligent about self-care. If you're not familiar with the term, self-care means creating a lifestyle that puts your sense of wholeness (mental/physical/spiritual/social) above everything else. It means you are intentional about making good choices for every aspect of your health.

It means I can't just ignore my pain or triggers and hope for the best. I cannot just keep up appearances. I cannot sweep things under the rug any longer. We've talked about a lot of these things in prior chapters, but this is where the rubber meets the road. This is where we put all those ideas and theories into practice.

I've heard people balk at the suggestion of starting a self-care routine, going to counseling, or investing in a life coach. Sometimes, it's because people view self-care as a selfish act. Especially if you've been around church leaders talking about "denying yourself" and only focusing on others, it can be tough to justify caring for yourself.

But self-care is letting yourself off the hook and trusting that the world will continue to spin on its axis, even if you aren't pushing. It's just like what flight attendants tell us at the beginning of every flight: make sure to put your oxygen mask on before you assist anyone else. If you pass out because you can't breathe, it will be impossible to take care of your kids, your commitments, or do the things you want to do.

Another reason people resist starting serious self-care is because they feel guilty about investing in themselves. But the only way to get something new (read: better) out of life is to stop settling for the same old things. If you want your life to change, you have to take actionable steps to make that happen. And often, you have to connect with an expert who knows how to help.

For you, that expert might be a nutritionist, life coach, or personal trainer. It could be a psychiatrist, counselor, or physical therapist. It might even be a professional organizer or a cleaning service to deep clean your house every few weeks. It doesn't matter what that looks like: you're worthy of investing in yourself.

If you have ever felt hopeless or believed that all the bad things in your life are beyond redemption, self-care is for you. If you have ever felt unworthy of being loved or accepted, it's time to create a self-care plan that works for *you.*

Remember your three lists from a few chapters ago? Use them here; they will help you look at your life and see what needs to change. If there are things on your "have to" list that can occasionally be outsourced to give yourself a break, do it. If there are things on your "want to" list that seem incredibly refreshing to you, pull out your schedule and write in time for them.

Self-care has saved my life and transformed me time and again. From the silent retreat that helped heal the brokenness of my marriage to learning to create healthy boundaries with toxic friends and family members, many forms of self-care have been part of my journey into calm. Self-care is personal. That's why it's called *self*—it's different for everyone. So what is it for you?

Self-Care Is...

Self-care helps you fight back against everything that pulls against your happiness, attention, and sense of self-worth. Self-care is giving yourself permission to say "no" to people, places, and things that make you feel unworthy or unsafe. Maybe it includes yoga, meditation, or exercise. For you, it might be centering prayers. For someone else, it could be massage therapy. (*I think I need to add that to my self-care routine a little more often.*)

Self-care is a big fat "hell no" to shame and a resounding "hallelujah" to everything that makes you feel loved, happy, safe, healthy, whole, valuable, at peace, motivated, connected, accepted, and wanted. Is that a local book club? A running group? A weekly night at the movies with a few friends? Snuggles with your sweet kids, early in the morning? Turning your phone off and looking into your spouse's eyes?

Self-care can be hard things, too. Going to therapy is tough, but worth it. And self-care might feel like walking into dilapidated rooms that house memories of all the bad things that have happened to you. It might hurt, but it empowers you to walk away from the pain and disappointment, to say goodbye to the haters and those who have hurt you the worst. Self-care gives you that little extra push to hold your head high, middle finger saluting the chaos, as you find more and more peace.

Self-Care & a Second Chance

It was 1:34 a.m. and I was awake with allergies. It was nothing new; itchy eyes, a scratchy throat, and a stuffy nose had plagued me for weeks. This particular night, I'd had enough. I headed to the kitchen for a glass of cold water and some help getting back to sleep. I knew the tiny allergy pill would help me get some rest and relief from my symptoms, so I slid my thumb under the arrow on the cap and popped open the bottle. As I tipped it over my palm, pink and white capsules spilled into my hand.

Then it happened. It was just a flash—a blink—and the image was gone. Still, it was enough to rattle me. For the first time in months, I was back in the hotel where I nearly died. I mean, my body was safely in my kitchen while my family slept upstairs. But my mind, my emotions, and my fight, flight, or freeze response were back inside that dreadful and desperate night.

During flashbacks, most people feel disconnected from themselves. It's hard to explain, but it might feel sort of like my head is separated from my body. Some people describe it as feeling lightheaded or dizzy or far away. That night, I shook my head to try to bring reality back into focus. I lost my footing, barely catching myself on the kitchen island before I hit the floor.

For half an hour, I reeled from the glimpse back into the night when my life hung in the balance. I saw the dingy hotel carpet, the bed behind me, the Bible on the pillow. I smelled the hot tea I used to mix my poison and drink it down. I felt the queasiness and the anxious rush to *just get it over with.*

What does self-care look like when you're still dealing with the aftermath of a crisis? What do you do when flashbacks still come, more stubbornly than you ever imagined? How do you handle the nightmares and heartache when you feel like you should be over it after all these years? Or the way you feel gutted every time you drop your kids off to visit their dad who left you for another woman? The grief that threatens to choke you when you're about to call that loved one to tell them about something funny and you realize you can't, because they're gone?

None of it is rational or reasonable. It's unfair and horrible. Maybe you're clinging to the voicemails you've saved, just to hear that loved one's voice, like I am since Boss died.

The circle of life sucks, no matter what Disney wants you to believe. *Bite me, Simba.* It is no fun to say goodbye to the ones we love dearly. I wanted my granddad to be free of his suffering. But I sure as hell would have preferred for him to get out of that damn hospital bed and live forever. I guess it's that way with all our heroes.

But he didn't get out of that hospital bed. He didn't live forever. And each time I drive up that long dirt road to visit Nanny, my heart breaks. Tears splash down my shirt as I ease down the driveway. I feel like the heavens should cry too, but they never seem to get the memo.

There are all sorts of hurts and I've shared plenty with you already. But this is the most profound pain I've felt in a long time. Chronic heartache. This is a loss that will never be recovered—a hole that cannot be filled. A dark cloud that rarely seems to lift.

When I think about self-care, I think about one of the many lessons the old newspaperman taught me when I was first getting into photography. He loved closeups. Whether I showed him a photograph of a face or a fencepost, it was never quite close enough to his liking. He always saw little distractions that could be cropped from the picture. Whether he was acting as a photographer, a writer, or a family man, Boss always showed me how to keep the main thing in focus.

He'd say, "Stevie, let's get it right down where the goats can eat it." He taught me to say what I mean. He taught me to get right down to what is most important, "down where the goats can eat it," and focus on that. Even in my heartache, I can hear this mentor of mine, this giant of my childhood, urging me to take care of myself. To keep what matters in focus.

I hear Boss's voice when I'm aching. He reminds me that, once the shock of a flashback or a wave of grief wears off and I realize what's happening, I have to acknowledge it before I can move on. I hold on through the roller coaster of memories and emotions, but I have to look at what's important and do what I can to process what has happened. For me, that means writing about it, just like Boss would have, because writing is a huge part of my self-care. But that will look different for you.

No two aches are the same. Whether it's grief, a flashback, a panic attack, or something else entirely, we can't avoid the hurt that leaves us reeling. But in those moments, the best thing we can do is breathe deep, grab the nearest seat (even if it's the floor) and tell ourselves we're okay. Because we *are* okay. We're just living through the hard stuff of life and need a little extra care.

Self-care during grief or healing from trauma seems complicated, but it's no different than any other time. Be gentle with yourself. Get help when you need it. Be honest about what you *really* need to do and give yourself lots and lots of grace.

We need to give ourselves time and space to process what has happened, whether it's losing a friendship or job or anything else. This way, we learn to handle the waves of pain and grief a little better each time they come up. The truth is, I am not the same desperate guy who tried to die by suicide in a hotel room kitchenette. I'm not the same guy I was a few months ago, before Boss died. I still hurt. I still miss him. I still get anxious sometimes. But I'm still learning to treat myself well. I'm still learning to take care of myself the way I would take care of those I love: with compassion and grace.

Life is Hard

My 5th-grade teacher, Terri Nobles, had a 2x4 in our classroom with the words "BOARD OF EDUCATION" written in black permanent marker. And if you failed to heed her warnings...no, she wouldn't whack you with it. (I know I grew up in the Alabama countryside, but we weren't *that* backwards!) Anyway, if you got in trouble, you'd find yourself at a picnic table during recess with that 2x4 and a piece of sandpaper, trying to get rid of the black permanent marker. It's shocking how deep permanent marker can sink into old pine.

You've probably guessed I spent my fair share of recesses with Mrs. Nobles hovering over me. I can still see her grin and hear her cackling in that *thick-as-molasses* Southern drawl.

"Steve Austin!" she'd say, "Life is hard, and then you die." (For those of you who haven't heard a true country drawl, she'd draw the word "life" out into about seven syllables. It was something like, "Laaaaaaaf is haarrd, an' then y'daaaaah.")

You laugh—or maybe you cringe at that story—but the principle isn't necessarily wrong. Growing up in Prosperity Gospel churches, it seemed most folks believed that the Christian life meant the end of suffering, pain, and hard times. We pictured God as some sort of cosmic Santa Claus, handing out health, wealth, and happiness to all the good little kids. But life just doesn't work that way, no matter how religious you are.

In this world, we are going to suffer. It's an unfortunate side effect of life. Terri Nobles is standing there, leaning over the picnic table of your life, saying, "Life is hard, and then you die." We want to *name it and claim it, believe it and receive it, blab it and grab it.* We think those truth-tellers are discouraging and depressing, but it doesn't have to be that way. After all, Jesus showed up on the scene and echoes the cry of all the realists: "In this world, you will have trouble" (John 16:33, NIV). He hands us the BOARD OF EDUCATION, while everybody else is playing, and whispers, "Life is hard..."

What if we reject all that name-it-and-claim-it crap and join Jesus and Terri Nobles? See, when we recognize that life is hard, we don't let any of those TV preachers tell us otherwise and shame us into hiding our pain. We refuse to shrink back from caring for ourselves and giving grace to others when we make peace with the fact that life is uncertain, unfair, and unpredictable.

"Life is suffering," said the Buddha, and Jesus responded, "Amen."

But that's not all they said. Buddha talked a whole lot about compassion. Jesus often talked about love and living something he called "abundant life." We can't truly experience any of those good things if we don't let ourselves feel and process the tough stuff, then make good self-care choices.

Yes, life beats us down, disappoints us, shocks us, makes us angry, and even leaves us feeling hopeless at times. This is why self-care is so important. We *must* intentionally carve out time to care for ourselves, so that we can handle the chaos of life. And I wonder if that's what Jesus meant when he finished his statement in John 16:33, "Take heart, I've overcome the world." What if that overcoming happens as we shift our mindsets and learn to love ourselves? Because it sure seems like it has for me.

Please learn from my experience. I'm a real guy who has walked through a living hell and has come out on the other side. I refuse to skirt the details of my story or pretend that life stops being hard once you're on the path from chaos to calm. Instead, I want you to know that a lifestyle of self-care can carry you through the hardest times. I've hit rock bottom and lived to tell about it. And even if you're nowhere near rock bottom, taking care of yourself is a necessary part of daily life. It will keep you holding on when everything else seems like too much.

eleven

WATCHING PORN WITH NANNY

*We must build our arks with love and ride out the storm
with courage and know that the little sprig of green in
the dove's mouth betokens a reality beyond the storm more
precious than the likes of us can imagine.*

—Frederick Buechner[32]

When I was in high school, I would drive over to Nanny and Boss's house in the country for Friday movie nights. It was pure heaven. Boss would cook banana pancakes or everything-but-the-kitchen-sink spaghetti. We watched these terribly fantastic B-movies like *Attack of the Killer Leeches, Swamp Thing, Animal House,* and *Porky's.*

After I moved to Lee University, I called and talked to Nanny and Boss several times a week. And I still made the three-hour drive home once a month to continue our movie night tradition. For several weeks, Nanny started telling me about this wonderful song called "Let the River Run." It played near the end of *Working Girl*[33] and she and Boss loved the music. They couldn't wait for me to hear the song the next time I was down for movie night.

From the time I got to their house, Nanny started warning me, "Now Stevie—there's this one little racy part that I'll need to fast-forward through, but don't worry. I've got the remote ready." She must have warned me ten times before we ever turned the movie on.

Once the movie started, Nanny was obviously nervous. Now, Nanny is not the most tech-savvy grandma in the South and she had an itchy trigger finger. She must have jumped to fast-forward the movie 27 times before we got to the scandalous scene. And then everything fell apart.

Suddenly, Nanny's trigger finger malfunctioned. Melanie Griffith was the working girl, and Alec Baldwin was getting *worked*. On screen. In explicit detail. Yeah, this movie was *definitely* rated R. Melanie Griffith's character looked much more like a rodeo cowgirl than a secretary. Got the image? *You're welcome.*

Nanny freaked the eff out. My sweet, saintly grandma started gasping and stammering and pressing every button on that remote control except fast-forward. When her fingers stopped mashing the buttons, they didn't stop the film. Instead, they landed on the pause button. There was nothing left to the imagination.

Nanny was in full-blown panic mode by this time, growling and stuttering and flushing a deeper blush than I'd ever seen. I had NEVER heard my grandfather laugh so hard. He was laid back in his recliner and I thought he might stop breathing.

In a desperate, last-ditch effort to protect her precious grandson (she probably *still* thinks I'm a virgin, even after a decade of marriage and two kids), Nanny started pressing buttons again. She managed to hit rewind, and I heard a soft whisper: *"Well, shit."* I couldn't believe my ears. Nanny had *never* sworn in my presence.

But sure enough, she said it again. "Shit." And then louder. "Shit. SHIT. *SHIT!!!*"

Again, she thought pressing buttons would fix it. So she pressed play. And the scene started over.

I nearly fell off the couch and peed my pants as a grown-ass man. I couldn't breathe. In the best possible way.

By this time, poor Nanny was so flustered that she threw her hands up in the air and joined Boss and me in uproarious laughter. We sat and watched the entire scene at regular speed. Together. Me and my grandparents. Watching softcore porn.

I had never laughed so hard.

The Sky is Falling

Sometimes, everything falls apart and you find yourself somewhere you never thought you'd be. Maybe you're not accidentally watching porn with your grandma. It might not be as funny as the time my mom innocently tried to sign GOOD MORNING to a deaf lady from church, but instead told her to SHOVE IT. (My family gives me *plenty* of reasons to laugh.)

Sometimes, like my mom, we make all these grand plans. We do the work, just like she practiced all week to be able to say hello to the sweet deaf lady. Everything can be rolling along just great as you try to do what's right or kind or wise. And things can still fall apart.

As you near the end of this book, know this: you can do all the work, follow all the suggestions, center yourself, meditate, exercise, connect with whatever type of everyday spirituality works for you, have a great support system, take your meds, and sometimes things will still fall apart. Sometimes, all the preparation in the world can't keep the sky from falling.

It doesn't mean there's anything wrong with you. Even the most spiritual people face the darkness. I know powerful and influential leaders who have felt crippled by stress and crushed by loss and shame. I think about Kay Warren, co-founder of Saddleback Church. Even though her husband has been touted as "America's Pastor," she's shared her brokenness as a mom who lost her precious son Matthew to suicide. Talking with Kay, I realized she and Rick had done *everything* they could for Matthew. They fought hard for him but still lost him. She told me, "There are parts of me that will never be completely healed."[34]

We've talked about how life is really hard sometimes and how crucial self-care is when you're walking through tragedy. In those moments, we come to know what Kay meant about never being completely healed. Some part may always carry the pain. But it's not a death sentence. It's an invitation to keep holding on. When things fall apart, as the waters of chaos churn all around us, there are four things we need to hold onto: hope, messy grace, love, and each other.

Hope

Before I started the recovery process six years ago, I considered driving my truck into the overpass countless times. There were days I drank, not for enjoyment, but out of desperation to numb the pain and anxiety. I know what it's like to write suicide notes. I can tell you about hopelessness.

Emily Dickinson said, "Hope is the thing with feathers that perches in the soul,"[35] but where is it when you've been blinded by disappointment, personal failure, or trauma? Where is hope when you believe, in the pit of your stomach, this will never get better? Where is your wishing star when the pain is so real that you can hardly imagine a miracle?

Hope is coming.

Hope is the resting place for abandoned wives and failed ministers. Hope is the dance floor for shattered dreams, long-since deferred. Hope is a promise that better days are coming.

Hope is the strength of an abuse survivor who finds courage to get the hell out. Hope is the endurance of a single mother who works a day job, goes to night school, and loves her children the best way she knows how. Hope is the wisdom of picking up a book that feeds your soul or calling a friend who can see the light you currently can't. Hope bends under the weight of chaos, but it doesn't break.

Hope is a gritting of the teeth,
a furrowing of the brows,
and a digging in of heels.
Hope is an anchor.

Storms suck. You get beat up, tossed around, and left wondering what in the world just happened. But the hope that better days are coming steadies me when seas swell and I am tumbled to and fro by waves of chaos. Hope might have feathers, but I think it's also the thing with claws that dig in when times are tough. It's wild-eyed and holds on because it is convinced that things will get better. Hope has lived through some crazy shit and knows that life sometimes just plain sucks. But Hope has been around long enough to know that things will get better. Hope is a stubborn refusal to give up on the promise that good days will come again.

Let me say it once more for the folks in the back: *Good days will come again.*

In time, the immediate and devastating chaos will subside and you'll be able to live in the present moment again. You'll even begin to look forward to what life brings your way. Better days are coming. Even if the present day feels like it might destroy you, hold on.

Like the tides of the ocean, Joy has washed over me when the hard days finally pass. That will happen for you, too. While we wait, Hope is both the anchor in the waves and the knot at the end of the rope to which we desperately cling. Joy is the message and Hope is the messenger. Hope washes in and out, like the ocean against my toes that cold New Year's weekend, reminding us again of the rhythm and the rhyme. All of life expands and contracts. We exhale—we lose our breath—but it always comes back with the inhale.

If you're stuck in the middle of a mess right now, I pray you hear the voice of Hope. That same voice has been whispering for eons, "Joy is coming." I can't promise when Joy will show up on your doorstep and the weeping will stop. But I know it always has for me.

I have to believe Joy will come again for you. And in Her arms, messy Grace.

Messy Grace

Life is messy. Parenting is messy. Recovery is messy. Just being a human means we're going to have to deal with some mess from time to time. But Grace is messy, too. And part of holding on means allowing Grace to embrace you, right in the midst of the mess.

Where do you see grace in your daily life? What words have been a balm for your soul? What song has lifted you from the mire? What image has caused your soul to dance? What I am most thankful for today is daily, tangible grace: the power of a second chance (or third, or fourth, or as many as it takes). The strength to get up and try again when Mike the Inner Critic is tearing you a new one. The compassion to let yourself off the hook when you feel like you've screwed up. It's all Grace, friend.

We are a seed, each one of us, capable of growing into something beautiful & powerful, able to impact the world with greatness. But sometimes that seed is covered with a lot of crap. Grace helps us dig through that crap, get silent, listen to our hearts, and discover the truth of our being: *anything is possible.* That's not some ridiculous motivational speech—it's the truth.

Extending Messy Grace to ourselves means we stop listening to lies that limit us. Instead, we dig deep to create a brand-new reality where we are cared for, accepted, and receive compassion. We're not just striving and surviving, but struggling to do our very-freakin-best to leave a mark on this old cold world. So give yourself an extra dose of Messy Grace today. Speak kindly to your soul. Try a little tenderness with yourself. Remember that everyone (including you) deserves another chance.

And everyone deserves Love.

Love

Dogma, doctrine, theology—Divine Love surpasses it all. What if Love was our entire theology, regardless of labels like atheist or Christian or whatever? What if the goal of our lives was to live and love as much as humanly possible? That's what I embrace about following Jesus. What if we listen to those who aren't exactly like us, with the goal of learning so that we can love better? What if Love was the goal?

> *"Love is from God; everyone who loves is born of God and knows God...for God is love."*
>
> —1 John 4:7-8, NIV

God is Love. But what does that even mean? One of the ways to better understand the nature of God is to better understand the nature of Love.

Love isn't only poetry; it is deeper than romance. Love doesn't care about your level of education. Love ain't concerned with grammar or syntax. Love's agenda isn't the exegesis of Scripture or the rightness of your theology. No one holds the corner market on Love.

Divine Love is stubborn AF and always in your corner. It doesn't care how many people you've "gotten saved," about your tax returns, or how many times you've dropped the ball. Love isn't counting your mistakes.

Love doesn't give a damn about what we say unless our actions match. Love isn't interested in our belief systems or spiritual laws, but always seeking to quietly out-serve the other.

Holding onto Love means finding it within yourself first. It is valuing relationship over everything else: relationship with yourself, with the Divine, with your people. It's investing in practices, places, and people that make you feel safe and accepted. It doesn't matter if it's a church or a gay bar, a synagogue or a roller-derby: hold onto the deep, safe, generous Love you find, wherever you find it.

Love is harmony. Love is the resting place between the notes that gives you time to catch your breath. And we need Love to hold onto each other.

Each Other

It's easy to feel overwhelmed by the darkness of human nature. Social media and cable news are full of discord. On bad days, it's enough to make us believe no one will ever understand us. We are too easily polarized by differences and paralyzed by fear. So we have to let go of the pseudo-community of social media. We have to find our tribe and hold onto our *real* people.

Finding a tribe is like building a puzzle. Separated, each tiny part of the whole doesn't make much sense. It's exciting to find a match for a single piece and realize it's not alone anymore. Still, it doesn't reveal much of the 1,000-part masterpiece, even when two or three pieces fit together. The big picture only starts to become clear as we continue to collaborate, connecting piece after piece.

When I look in the mirror, I see just one piece of God. We need each other for the Divine to make sense, just like we need each puzzle piece to see the picture. As we embrace the richness of our various colors and flavors in community, our collective soul sighs, "*This is good.*"

In his book, *You are Here,* Thich Nhạt Hanh says:

> *To me, the definition of hell is simple. It is a place where there is no understanding and no compassion. We have all been to hell. We are acquainted with hell's heat, and we know that hell is in need of compassion. If there is compassion, then hell ceases to be hell.*[36]

And don't we know what that's like? We thrive on relationship and desperately need each other. We're all wishing for someone to glance our way, offer a smile of solidarity, and acknowledge that we are doing our very best. And when we experience that simple compassion, don't the fires of chaos die down?

So, who loves you unconditionally and puts up with your trauma and drama? Do they also tell you the truth, even when it's uncomfortable? Who encourages you and allows you to vent, but cares enough about you to help you see a different perspective? Who are your safe people?

Hold onto your tribe, both when you're experiencing chaos and when you can share a little calm. We create space for belonging within ourselves and space at the table for others. As we embrace a life of Messy Grace, we are doing the transformative work of creating heaven where there has previously been hell.

Keep Holding On

If you're in a rough patch and it feels like nothing is working, let me remind you one last time: hard times come and go, just like the tides. Sometimes shitty days turn into shitty weeks and months, but they don't last forever. Chaos says, "What goes up won't stay there long." Calm shouts back when we're shaky-scared, "But what goes down must come up." Chaos shows up, but it won't be too long before calm pushes it back. When bad news arrives, take a deep breath and look back on all the bad news you've already lived through. You are stronger than you think.

So keep hoping. Keep holding on when life serves up a shit sandwich. When Mike the Inner Critic starts running his dirty little mouth, keep trusting that better days are coming. Keep looking for goodness and beauty. Keep your eyes peeled for Love to show up. Sooner or later, it will. Eventually, the tide will recede, the waters will calm, and you will have gained new strength and new wisdom for the journey.

The world groans under the weight of its own brokenness, but Hope keeps holding on. In the midst of hell breaking loose in our personal lives, we are the keepers of our inner peace. We might be heartbroken, but wild-eyed Hope digs her claws in, confident that life will get better. One day, our waiting will be worth it.

Sometimes chaos still shows up for me. But mindfulness, self-care, silencing the inner critic, embracing everyday spirituality, and being frugal with my Give a Damns have allowed my life to blossom in ways I never imagined. Life isn't always comfortable, but I have the tools to get through the pain. I'm not silly enough to think there won't be more thorny patches along my path, but I know that there will be blossoms, too.

In the dark Valley of the Overwhelmed, the shadows loom, the wind howls, and the rains come. But keep on walking. One step at a time. Crawl if you have to. Because just around the bend, if you remain patient and determined, you'll find the air is turning clear and crisp again. Catch your breath: you don't have to be overwhelmed any longer.

Steve Austin

ABOUT THE AUTHOR

 **STEVE AUSTIN** was a pastor when he nearly died by suicide. A second chance, a grueling recovery, and years of honest conversation allowed Steve to find healing and purpose. It's evident in his writing, speaking, podcasting, and coaching: he helps overwhelmed people get their lives back.

Steve is also the author of the Amazon bestseller *From Pastor to a Psych Ward*. He lives in Birmingham, Alabama, with his wife, Lindsey, and their two children. Find him online at iamsteveaustin.com.

STAY CONNECTED

- Download the study guide for FREE! Just go to catchingyourbreathbook.com.
- Listen to the #AskSteveAustin Podcast at AskSteveAustin.com.
- Read Steve's blog (and sign up for his free weekly newsletter) at iAmSteveAustin.com.
- Invite Steve to speak. Steve is available to speak to groups of all ages about subjects, including: self-care, suicide prevention, wholeness, and how to catch your breath.

Interested in life coaching or spiritual direction?
Visit iamsteveaustin.com/coaching today!

NOTES

1   Stevenson, Bryan. *Just Mercy: A Story of Justice and Redemption*. Melbourne: Scribe, 2016.
2   Stanton, Andrew, and Lee Unkrich, dirs. 2003. *Finding Nemo*. DVD. Burbank, CA: Buena Vista Pictures.
3   Zemeckis, Robert. *Forrest Gump*. (Los Angeles, California: Paramount, 1994)
4   Dyer, Dr. Wayne. *There is a Spiritual Solution to Every Problem*. New York. HarperCollins Publishers, 2001.
5   Sexton, Anne. "Despair." Accessed May 16, 2018. https://www.poemhunter.com/poem/despair-7
6   Balram, Devin. "Weak Sometimes." Accessed May 16, 2018. https://noisetrade.com/devinbalram
7   O'Connor, Flannery, *The Letters of Flannery O'Connor: The Habit of Being*, edited by Sally Fitzgerald. New York: Farrar, Straus, and Giroux, 1988.
8   Dictionary.com, "agnostic." access July 21, 2018. http://www.dictionary.com/browse/agnostic/unique?s=t
9   Hazleton, Lesley. *Agnostic: A Spirited Manifesto*. Riverhead Books, 2017.
10   "The Good or the Real," Chrishala Lishomwa, accessed May 16, 2018, http://symphonyforlove.blogspot.com/2016/08/the-good-or-real-by-chishala-lishomwa.html.
11   Brené Brown, "Own our History. Change the Story," accessed May 16, 2018, https://brenebrown.com/blog/2015/06/18/own-our-history-change-the-story/.
12   Anne Lamott, "Becoming the Person You Were Meant to Be: Where to Start," *O, The Oprah Magazine,* November, 2009.
13   "Secrets," Lola Ridge, accessed May 17, 2018, https://www.poets.org/poetsorg/poem/secrets-0.
14   Mike Foster and Jennifer Foster, *Five Dates* (San Diego, CA: Foster Resources, 2017).
15   Hanh, Thich Nhat. Call Me by My True Names: The Collected Poems of Thich Nhat Hanh. Berkeley, CA: Parallax Press, 1999.
16   Dictionary.com, "unique," accessed May 17, 2018, http://www.dictionary.com/browse/unique?s=t.
17   Howard Thurman, occasion unidentified. This often-used quotation is attributed to Reverend Thurman on the history page of the Howard Thurman Center for Common Ground at Boston University, https://www.bu.edu/thurman/about/history/.
18   "Mark Twain on England," Mark Twain, accessed May 16, 2018, http://www.twainquotes.com/Criticism.html.
19   Denise Jacobs, *Banish Your Inner Critic.* (Coral Gables, FL: Mango Publishing Group, 2017).
20   "Let Go," Jennifer Williamson, accessed May 16, 2018, http://aimhappy.com/.
21   *Dictionary.com,* "overwhelmed," accessed May 17, 2018, http://www.dictionary.com/browse/overwhelmed?s=t.
22   "Letters to a Young Poet," Rainer Maria Rilke, accessed May 16, 2018, https://www.goodreads.com/author/quotes/7906.Rainer_Maria_Rilke.

23   Messina, Jo Dee, writer. "My Give a Damn's Busted." In *Delicious Surprise*. Curb Records, 2005, CD.

24   The Eagles. "Take It Easy." In *The Studio Albums: 1972-1979*. Warner Strategic Marketing, 2013, CD.

25   Marc Alan Schelske, *The Wisdom of Your Heart: Discovering the God-Given Purpose and Power of Your Emotions* (Colorado Springs, CO: David C. Cook, 2017), 127, 144.

26   Bottum, J. Carroll. "Increasing Farmers Understanding of Public Problems and Policies." *Journal of Farm Economics* 37, no. 5 (1955). 1307.

27   "Keeping Quiet," Pablo Neruda, accessed May 17, 2018, accessed http://www.sfcenterforselfcompassion.com/poetry/.

28   Manning, Brennan, John Blase, and Jonathan Foreman. *Abbas Child: The Cry of the Heart for Intimate Belonging*. Colorado Springs, CO: NavPress, 2015.

29   Ed Bacon, *8 Habits of Love: Overcome Fear and Transform Your Life* (New York: Grand Central Life & Style, 2012).

30   Garcia-Rill, E. "Reticular Activating System." *Encyclopedia of Neuroscience*, 2009, 137-43. Accessed July 31, 2018. doi:10.1016/c2009-1-03742-3.

31   Oliver, Mary. *Blue Pastures*. New York: Houghton Mifflin Harcourt Publishing Company, 1995.

32   Buechner, Frederick. *The Hungering Dark*. San Francisco: Harper, 1991.

33   *Working Girl*. Performed by Alec Baldwin and Melanie Griffith. 1988. VHS.

34   Kay Warren, "There are parts of me that will never be completely healed." *CXMH*, Podcast, September 10, 2017, audio, 53:30. https://cxmhpodcast.com/show-notes/2017/9/7/19-feat-kay-warren.

35   Dickinson, Emily. "Hope." *The Poems of Emily Dickinson*. Ralph W. Franklin (ed.). Cambridge, MA: Belknap Press, 1999.

36   Hanh, Thich Nhat. *You Are Here*. Reprint Edition. Shambala. 2010.